Ellen Roseman's Money Guide for Modern Families

Ellen Roseman's Money Guide for Modern Families

Ellen Roseman

Ellen Roseman

Doubleday Canada Limited

Canadian Cataloguing in Publication Data

Roseman, Ellen, 1947-
Ellen Roseman's money guide for modern families

ISBN 0-385-25502-0

1. Finance, Personal.
I. Title. II. Title: money guide for modern families.

HG179.R67 1995 332.024 C94-932715-8

Cover design by Terry O Communications
Cover photographs by Johnnie Eisen
Printed and bound in the USA

Published in Canada by
Doubleday Canada Limited
105 Bond Street
Toronto, Ontario
M5B 1Y3

Thank you to Darlene Gres for research; Beatrice Fischer for providing an office; financial planner Janet Freedman and lawyer Barry Corbin for reading the manuscript and suggesting changes; and Joanne Thomas Yaccato, Marina Strauss, Alexandra Eadie and Wendy Barnes for friendship and moral support.

In recognition of the fact that not all families have the financial resources to plan for the future, a portion of the author's royalties on the sale of this book will go to Campaign 2000, a coalition of fifty groups across Canada dedicated to eliminating child poverty.

Table of Contents

Introduction ix

1 Becoming a Couple 1

2 Separation, Divorce and Remarriage 31

3 Stitching Your Safety Net 59

4 As Your Parents Get Older 95

5 Raising a Family 125

6 Saving for Your Child's Education 147

7 Teaching Your Children About Money 175

Bibliography 197

Index 199

Introduction

In July, 1994, *Money* magazine profiled a family in Grass Lake, Michigan, a small town west of Detroit. The husband worked as a quality analyst in a General Motors transmission plant, earning just over $40,000 a year, and the wife looked after their dozen offspring, ranging from one to seventeen years old. The family managed remarkably well on one paycheque, taking few vacations, rarely dining out and eating at home on a skimpy grocery bill of just $125 a week. Devout Catholics, they shared simple values: "There's no whining about missed trips to Disney World or pleading for allowances, which their parents can't afford," the magazine said.

I saved the article and I look at it every time I feel hassled by kids' demands and money woes. The gang of eight girls and four boys—all single births, no twins—are so wholesome. And there's a poignant shot of the 37-year-old wife in the basement, baby in one arm, laundry basket in the other, clothes strewn over the floor. "Basically, my whole day is laundry," she says. Not only does she hang her washing outside on sunny days to reduce electricity use, but she's a ferocious cents-off coupon clipper, filing her finds by category in a red plastic lunch box.

Once the norm, this type of family has become so unusual that it invokes wonder and pity in readers of the 1990s. Today's families are smaller and most have two incomes. The spouses are not always married to each other and sometimes are the same sex. The children often have other parents than the ones they live with. In a time of bewildering social change, you can't make easy assumptions any more about Mom and Dad and the kids.

My own family appears traditional at first. My husband, Edward Trapunski, and I are on our first marriage and have two sons of our own. Yet he is self-employed and works at home, trying to focus on projects and sound professional with youngsters screaming and playing in the background. When there's a crisis at school or an emergency home repair, he's the one who takes the call. His income fluctuates, while my job pays the mortgage and provides the health benefits we count on. It's a role reversal we're not always comfortable with, but that's life in the modern world.

No matter what the complexion of your family or mine, the financial issues we face are pretty much the same. Few of us have enough money to go around, nor have we bothered to set up an emergency fund, write a will or update our insurance coverage. Many of us are sandwiched between young children and aging parents, trying to provide for their needs while saving what we can for our own retirement. We want to teach our kids to be responsible and have good money habits, and we hope they don't make the stupid mistakes we did.

The way we implement our financial goals will vary. The division of property after divorce or death, for example, is different for married couples than for those living in a common-law or same-sex relationship or in a blended family. The safety net we need depends on whether we work for a large company, a small company or our own company. There are as many methods of saving for a child's education as there are schools to choose from.

This book tries to tailor advice to modern families in all their diversity. My goal was to include as many types of relationships as possible, though I realize it's impossible to do justice to everyone. As a personal finance writer, I used to get angry at advisors who assumed the husband was the primary wage-earner and the wife stayed home or worked just enough to retain her dependent status for tax purposes. I wanted to shake them out of their complacency and tell them the nuclear family is no longer the model. Today, most women earn money and some of us outearn our male partners. With changing social values, the old norms do not apply.

Money is still a big issue and will probably continue to be. In a survey published in June, 1994, *Worth* magazine asked 2,000 people what they fight about most with their partners. The top answer was whether to spend or save money, followed by what TV programs to watch and how to discipline the kids. Arguments about their sex life ranked far down on most people's list. And when asked what they think about more often on an average day, 40 per cent said money and only 13 per cent said sex.

Writing this book, though hard work, was more fun than I had imagined. I cannot thank my family enough for their love and support. Edward's enduring presence on the home front makes it possible for me to do what I do, for which I am grateful. Our two boys, Charles, 13, and Richard, 8, are demanding but always a delight. Their daily insights give us an enchanting view of a child's world. My parents, David and Connie Roseman in Montreal, are a source of strength and wise counsel.

I want to thank *The Globe and Mail*, my employer for almost 20 years, for giving me the freedom to grow as a columnist. I was the first to write as a consumer advocate in the newspaper's front section and later in the Report on Business. My editors have let me say what I wanted most of the time, though the topic of babies was banned for a while.

In hindsight, I admit I got carried away by the birth of my first child and wrote endlessly about cribs, bottles, diapers and car seats. (One reader said his favourite feature, after sports, was Ellen Roseman's "My Life with Charles.") Peggy Wente, my editor since 1990, has let me take on a variety of interesting jobs and didn't begrudge me the time involved in doing the book.

My literary and speaker's agent, David Lavin, encouraged me to tackle this topic. He felt strongly that there was a niche for a personal finance guide for families and brought a high level of enthusiasm to Doubleday, which backed this project admirably. Working with editors like John Pearce and Maggie Reeves has been a pleasure. I hope the book will be useful to readers and that your comments and questions will be included in future editions.

1 BECOMING A COUPLE

You meet someone, you fall in love, you settle down together. Before you know it, you're a couple—whether or not the union was formalized with a legal or religious service. You have talked about a million things, but money may not be one of them. Sure, each of you probably knows how much the other earns and what credit cards you carry. But have you seriously discussed how you will share your finances? Will you pool your money or keep separate accounts? Who will look after which expenses? These are some of the hardest questions couples face; ones that, if not confronted and resolved, can weaken the bonds that tie them.

There is no one answer that fits every couple. As the relationship evolves, you find an arrangement that works for you and plays to each other's strengths. Ideally, both partners should know what is going on, even if only one handles the money. But we all know couples who don't live up to the ideal, who have old-style marriages in which one partner is a financial illiterate and happily hands over responsibility to the other. This is far from the best solution, but it may be the most suitable one for them.

In her book *Double Income Families,* Winnipeg financial planner Lynne MacFarlane cites the example of scientist and broadcaster David Suzuki, who leaves all money-related matters to his wife, Tara Cullis. He doesn't even carry a cheque book. "For the Suzukis, it works, and you can't argue with success," says Ms. MacFarlane. "The important thing is that this family has made a choice."

But many couples slide into financial arrangements that please neither partner. Resentment builds, fights erupt, tears ensue—but the spark may have nothing to do with money. Disagreements about petty issues may escalate because of the dissatisfaction partners feel about their ill-fitting or unequal financial roles. That's why it's important to get everything on the table at an early stage, rather than waiting till roles have crystallized.

People going into second marriages are often more up-front about money than those settling down for the first time. That's why a legally binding marriage contract is more common when spouses have been married before. But even with unions that occur later in life, many people feel that talking about money is like throwing ice water on the romance. They find the whole idea distasteful.

This chapter will look at the major financial issues that affect people in relationships, whether married, remarried, common-law or same-sex unions. It will discuss sharing money and property, domestic contracts, taxes, pensions and benefits, wills and estate planning.

Sharing Money and Property

In the families many of us grew up in, the husband earned all the money and handed over enough to his wife to pay for the grocery bills and miscellaneous household expenses. If she was a shrewd shopper—and most housewives were—she hoarded money in a cookie jar or special account to indulge herself and her children. Chances are the husband never knew or heard about the secret stash.

Today, men are no longer the sole providers. Most women spend time in the work force and earn money of their own, even if they take a few years off to stay home and care for young children. They are used to paying bills, making major purchases like cars and homes and investing for the future. In some families, women are the primary wage earners. Tell these women to leave the financial decisions to the men in their lives and they will flee for the exit doors.

So, modern couples have to decide whether to combine their finances or keep them apart. Money talk, as always, leads into discussions of other issues—what you want out of life, what things are important to you and how you want to spend your time. It's important to examine and share your feelings and not keep them bottled up. Money issues are issues of power and control that touch on every aspect of a relationship, including your sex life.

There are an infinite numbers of ways to manage money together. The one you feel comfortable with depends on your financial resources, your attitudes toward saving and spending, and your desire for independence or interdependence. In her book, Lynne MacFarlane isolates five popular approaches:

- **The pool.** All earnings go into a common account and all bills and spending allowances are paid out of this pool. This arrangement works well when both partners earn about the same amount, have roughly the same goals and agree to merge everything.
- **Equal contributions.** Both partners put the same amount into a pot to cover joint expenses, but each person also has a personal savings and chequing account. They agree in advance on what expenses should be pooled and what should be kept separate. Again, this is appropriate when both salaries are the same.
- **Proportionate contributions.** Each partner puts a certain percentage of his or her income into the pool. If both contribute 50 per cent of their pay, the person making

$50,000 after tax puts $25,000 into the pool. If the other person makes $30,000 after tax, he or she puts in $15,000. This method is usually fairer when salaries are different and works well when incomes vary wildly from year to year.

- **Splitting the bills.** This is the method Edward and I use, in which each of us is responsible for paying certain bills. The mortgage and utility payments come out of my bank account, while he pays for restaurant meals and vacations. This approach works well when partners prefer to pay for specifics, rather than pooling money, but ongoing discussions are needed to allocate expenses fairly.
- **Month-by-month approaches.** One partner pays all the bills each month, then adds up the total and gets reimbursed for half the amount by the other. This works when one person enjoys paying bills and keeping accounts straight and the other doesn't. Another way to do it is to let both partners pay joint bills. At the end of the month, totals are tallied and the one who paid less writes a cheque to the other for the difference to even things out. This method definitely requires more bookkeeping.

Whatever method you choose—and there are as many methods as there are couples—both partners should feel the division is fair and each is paying his or her share of family expenses. If there is a difference in spending styles—say, for example, one person is extravagant and the other is tightfisted—both of you should sit down and figure out how much you need to pay the bills and save for the goals that are important to you. If there is money left over, the frugal partner should not resent the other's occasional indulgences.

"Everyone should have at least some money he doesn't have to account for," says Toronto financial planner David

Stewart. I wholeheartedly agree. My mother and mother-in-law both stayed home to raise families. Their first taste of financial independence came when they turned 65 and started getting their old age pension. Luckily, today's women don't have to wait that long—and their relationships are more egalitarian as a result.

Once how to pay the monthly bills is settled, couples can go on to discuss other financial issues. Should you have joint or individual credit card accounts? How much life insurance do you need? Should you merge savings and investments or keep them apart? It makes sense to pool investments, "so there's a balanced holistic approach that also takes into account the tax consequences," says Ron Trace, a financial planner with KPMG Peat Marwick Thorne in Toronto. But some people prefer the independence of managing their own portfolio. I certainly do.

Marriage Contracts

Your discussions about money can become the basis of a prenuptial agreement or marriage contract. Just as a will determines how you want your assets distributed at death, a domestic contract determines how your assets are to be divided if the relationship breaks down. The contract can override provincial family law provisions so that, on separation or divorce, your assets can be dealt with as you have decided they will be, rather than as the province has legislated.

In many provinces, it is also possible for unmarried couples who are living together to sign a legally binding cohabitation agreement, which determines how their property will be divided. Having a written contract is even more important for cohabiting couples than for married couples, because at present there are no laws to ensure an unmarried partner gets a share of the other's house, business or pension on separation or death.

Do you need a marriage contract? Edward and I had one prepared by a notary before our 1974 wedding, then put it in a drawer (as many people do) and never referred to it again. For us, it was irrelevant. Young couples entering into first marriages with no children and few assets probably can live without a contract. But when you own stuff that is important to you—even if it isn't worth much—you may feel better writing down who gets the china if you split, who gets the stereo equipment and who gets custody of the dog. And some couples like to formalize their arrangement for sharing responsibility for household expenses during the marriage.

Though still uncommon, marriage contracts are used when one partner has a lot more money than the other. Wealthy parents often insist that a young couple work out a financial agreement to prevent family money from going to the other spouse in a divorce. People who have been through a divorce are more likely to see the need for a contract. A man or woman with a thriving business, for example, may want to protect it from marital claims, after being burned in a previous marriage. A woman may want to preserve clear title to a house from a former husband, for the sake of her kids.

Like a will, a marriage contract does not have to be drafted by a lawyer (but it does have to be signed and witnessed). Nevertheless, each partner should get independent legal advice to make sure the terms are fair to both. Failure to get independent legal advice can lead to the contract's being set aside by a court, since the parties didn't understand what was signed. If you sign a contract before you get married, consult a lawyer a few months ahead to leave time for evaluating assets and negotiating. You can also sign at any time during a marriage but with far less leverage.

Lawyers are often consulted about marriage contracts, but the contract is left unsigned when issues touch a nerve close to home. Michael Cochrane, a family lawyer in Toronto, says the best way to resolve disputes is to ask why a specific asset—a home, a business, a pension—is to be excluded from the division of property in a separation or divorce.

Sometimes, a spouse wants to hang on to antiques or artworks that were inherited or have great sentimental value. In the case of a business, the owner's partners or lenders may insist that the spouse sign away any claims to company assets. The fear is that the company won't have enough cash to settle the claim and may have to be liquidated or sold if the marriage breaks down.

There are ways to ensure that one spouse is not disadvantaged, says Mr. Cochrane in a helpful book, *Surviving Divorce: The Everyday Guide for Canadians.* "Perhaps the spouse with the home can take out an irrevocable insurance policy payable to the other spouse," he says. And a spouse asked to give up a claim in a business can substitute a full interest in another asset. For example, the wife releases her claim on the husband's business and he releases any interest in the family home. If a separation occurs, he keeps the business and she keeps the house.

Another feature you can include in a marriage contract is the level of financial support for a spouse after divorce. The partners may agree not to ask for support from each other, or they may agree to an actual monthly amount and a fixed term, say $500 a month for 18 months. Obviously, the amount has to be updated regularly, but every amendment means all legal formalities must be complied with and there is no guarantee that both spouses will agree to changes later on. If possible, a formula at the outset will be worth considering. Couples can also include how they will divide responsibility for household chores and child care.

There are some things you cannot put into a marriage contract—or if you do, they will not be binding on anyone or the court. For example, a couple cannot provide for custody of or access to their children after separation, since the child's best interests cannot be ascertained in advance. Similarly, attempts to fix or avoid child support are not binding. However, you can agree to certain childrearing methods, such as education or religious instruction. In Ontario and some other provinces, you can't bargain away your right of possession of a matrimonial home or your right to consent to its sale or mortgaging.

Like other legal documents, a marriage contract should be reviewed regularly because circumstances change. Children are born, property is sold, illnesses develop and career changes are made. A couple who agreed to have separate property at the outset of a marriage may find themselves in an awkward situation 15 years later if one of them has given up a career to raise children, says Mr. Cochrane. "The contract is still binding on them and will have accomplished little if it only produces a patently unfair result for one of them." If you move to another province, state or country, get a lawyer there to check out the contract because the laws may be substantially different.

Cohabitation Agreements

If you are unmarried and living together with a partner of the opposite sex, you can sign a legally binding cohabitation agreement (in most provinces) in which you agree to the same matters as married spouses do. It's vitally important to set guidelines on dividing your property, since common-law spouses have no statutory property rights in Canada—and that comes as a surprise to many people.

Mr. Cochrane spoke to dozens of people, including lawyers, who thought that once you met the provincial definition of common-law spouse, you were automatically entitled to every right available to a legally married spouse. The prevalence of that view prompted him to write his legal guide. "It doesn't matter if a man and woman live together for fifty years," he stresses. "If they do not marry, the only property they are entitled to when they leave is their own property."

What if the common-law spouses acquired property together? Then the courts will look at their intentions and financial contributions and try to achieve a fair split that does not enrich one partner at the expense of the other. Each case is different, and the size of an unmarried partner's interest in a piece of property will depend on the facts of the particular case.

A cohabitation agreement will spell out in advance what happens to joint purchases or investments if you separate or one of you dies. You can agree to divide all property equally; to divide only the types of property you identify as family assets; to keep separate the property that one spouse paid for and is registered in his or her name; or to be treated as if you were legally married and thus covered by the provincial family law for property division.

Even without a contract, you may be entitled to financial support after a common-law union ends. (Most provinces recognize this right, except Quebec and the Northwest Territories.) The court will consider how long you lived together and whether one partner was dependent on the other. If you qualify for support, the amount to be paid and the time period will be calculated in the same way as for legally married spouses who have separated.

If you have a cohabitation agreement, you can provide for spousal support in the same way as a marriage contract does. That is, says Mr. Cochrane, you can waive support or fix it according to your wishes. Like married couples, common-law couples cannot make advance provisions for their children's support but can agree to educational and religious training. If the partners later get married, the cohabitation agreement will turn into a marriage contract.

Suppose that, despite all your good intentions, things fall apart. Can your marriage or cohabitation agreement be thrown out by the courts? Yes, says Mr. Cochrane, though it happens rarely and in limited circumstances. A domestic contract may be invalid if one person failed to disclose an important asset, or misunderstood the nature of the contract.

However, it's hard to plead ignorance if you received independent legal advice and signed a statement that you understood what you were doing and were doing so voluntarily.

Same-Sex Couples

So far, legislation has remained silent on whether people of the same sex living together as a couple can sign a binding cohabitation agreement. In any province, if a same-sex relationship ends in separation or death, the partners don't have any of the rights of married partners—such as the sharing of property and financial support. However, if a partner contributed financially or by work to the acquisition of property, he or she can sue for compensation based on the principle that one person should not be unjustly enriched by the work of another.

After death, unmarried and same-sex partners are not entitled to inherit each other's property. That is why it is important to draft a will, since, with some exceptions, you can leave your property to whomever you want by will. To avoid problems of interpretation, however, you should identify a former cohabiting partner by name rather than status. If two people of the opposite sex living together later marry, an existing will is automatically revoked by the marriage.

Same-sex couples are going to court, using the federal Charter of Rights and provincial human rights laws, to seek the same protection and benefits that are available to married couples and unmarried couples of the opposite sex. These include pensions, welfare, workers' compensation, health and dental benefits and tax advantages. The case law is still scanty, but things are improving for same-sex couples as awareness builds.

There are also many non-romantic couples living together—say a mother and adult daughter, uncle and nephew, brother and sister, or long-time friends. Generally, they do not have any legal rights to property when a relationship ends in separation or death. But if one person was clearly dependent on the other, the dependent may be able to sue for support or make a claim on the estate, no matter what the will says. However, successful cases of this kind are few and far between.

Minimizing Taxes

In the past, common-law couples—especially those with two incomes—received different tax treatment than married couples. That unfairness was eliminated when the federal government amended the Income Tax Act on January 1, 1993. Now, unmarried couples of the opposite sex are treated the same way as married couples for tax purposes. So there are no longer any monetary benefits to cohabiting or to being married.

You and your partner are considered spouses for tax purposes if you have lived together in a conjugal relationship for at least 12 months or have had a child together. The question everyone wants to know is how the federal government will monitor common-law couples. The answer: It's not clear.

Marriage, separation and divorce are legally defined by paperwork (registration, separation agreements, divorce decrees), but there are no documents to sign when a common-law relationship begins and ends. Even the partners may not know how long they have been together. For what it's worth, the government says that if a couple has lived apart for 90 days because of a breakdown in their relationship, they are no longer deemed to be spouses.

There are some advantages for unmarried couples in the new tax regime. They include:

- You can contribute to a registered retirement savings plan for a common-law partner. This is helpful if one partner has a lower income and lower RRSP limit. If the other contributes to a spousal plan, the couple can split income and save taxes when taking money out of their RRSPs in retirement.
- If one spouse has an annual income of $6,000 or less, the other spouse can claim the married credit.

- Medical expenses and charitable donations can be lumped together and claimed by either spouse. Also, unused tax credits for tuition fees, moving expenses, disability, old age, pensions and dividends can be transferred between spouses.
- You can leave assets to a common-law spouse after you die without attracting capital gains tax. Say you have a large amount in an RRSP, which you leave to your spouse. He or she will get a tax-free rollover of the RRSP. Before the law changed, your estate paid tax on the RRSP at its current market value and your common-law spouse received what was left after tax.

For most unmarried couples, the following disadvantages probably outweigh the advantages:

- You can have only one principal residence between the two of you. This means if each partner owns a house, only one gets a tax-free capital gain when the property is sold. For 1992 and earlier years, the principal residence exemption was available to each common-law spouse. To make it worse, Ottawa wiped out the $100,000 capital gains exemption for second properties just before this change took effect.
- You cannot claim the equivalent-to-spouse tax credit if you have a dependent child living at home. This used to give you the same tax savings as if you were supporting a spouse.
- Your income will be added to your spouse's to see if you qualify to receive the child tax benefit, the GST credit and provincial tax credits.
- If you have children living with you, you can't claim the child care expense deduction on the basis of separate incomes to maximize refunds. Child care expenses must be claimed by the spouse with the lower income.

- If you give money or investments to a common-law spouse, you will have to pay tax on any interest earned. If you sell property, any capital gain on the sale will be attributed back to you for tax purposes. As a result, the opportunities to split income between common-law spouses are greatly reduced.

With the new rules for common-law spouses, some tax inequities have disappeared. But others remain. For example, Canada's tax law favours double-income families and discriminates against married or common-law families in which one spouse earns all the income. This unfairness hits particularly hard when women leave the paid work force, at least temporarily, to raise children.

Take two couples, A and B, each of whose family income is $64,400. (This figure is used to simplify some of the calculations.) The husband of couple A earns all the income and he pays total tax of about $19,450. In the case of couple B, both spouses work, each earning $32,200. Each spouse pays roughly $7,380 in tax, for a total of $14,760. The difference between the two couples' tax bills? A hefty $4,690.

Such a disparity does not exist in the United States, where couples are allowed to file joint tax returns, says Toronto chartered accountant Colleen Gibb. In the above example, filing a joint return would have the effect of reducing couple A's taxes or increasing couple B's taxes.

The child care expense deduction also discriminates against one-income couples. Eligible wage earners can claim child care expenses of up to $5,000 a year for each child under seven, and up to $3,000 a year for each child seven to 14. Assume our couples each has one child under seven. Couple A, where the wife is at home, will not see their tax situation change. Even if they pay for child care so the wife can be an active volunteer or work as an artist or writer earning a low net income, no deduction is allowed.

Couple B gets the deduction. If they qualify for the full $5,000, their taxes are reduced to a total of about $13,020 (from $14,760). Now they pay $6,430 less in tax than couple A.

Of course, as Ms. Gibb rightly points out, $5,000 doesn't cover the cost of day care in many communities. Couple B may have to hire a nanny, at an out-of-pocket cost of $12,000 a year. Only $5,000 is deductible, and the tax refund in the top bracket is only $2,500. The other $9,500 must come out of their own after-tax income. And that's another problem with the tax system.

Splitting Income

So, how do you go about minimizing taxes? If you are part of a household in which one partner is taxed at the top marginal tax rate and the other is taxed at the lowest marginal rate or pays no tax at all, you can lower your overall tax burden by splitting income with your spouse. These income-splitting opportunities—though limited because Ottawa has been clamping down in the past few years—are not usually available to couples with two equal incomes.

For example, you can arrange your finances so that the higher-income spouse pays as many of the living expenses as possible. The other spouse saves or invests the money, and pays tax at his or her lower rate on the interest earned. The tax savings can be significant. A couple earning $1,000 in annual interest will net only $500 or so after tax if the spouse with the higher income claims it. The same amount of interest is worth $700 to $750 to the lower-income spouse.

A number of tax credits are transferable between spouses. The lower-income spouse should always claim these credits to reduce his or her tax liability as much as possible. The tax saved can be invested and the income generated will be taxed at a lower rate than it would be in the hands of the higher-bracket spouse.

If there is any tax owing by the lower-income spouse, the other spouse should pay it. The money that would otherwise be used to pay income taxes will be available for savings or investment—and the interest will be taxed in the hands of the lower-income spouse.

One of the best ways to split income is if one of you has your own business. Then you can hire your spouse to work for you and pay a regular salary. (The salary must be reasonable for the work performed, of course.) If your spouse is a full-time homemaker, there are additional benefits to earning a salary, such as paying into CPP and contributing to an RRSP, which will later provide a retirement income.

Also, you can give or lend money to your spouse to buy an interest in a business (including his or her own business or your business) and the resulting income will be taxed in his or her hands, not yours. Make sure the business is bona fide and your spouse is an active partner, not just a passive investor. An investment dealer once put together a limited partnership in which people could invest in a mortgage portfolio. The way it was structured, it fit the definition of business income. But the government said it was not really a legitimate business and did not qualify.

Spousal RRSPs

A popular way to split income is to contribute to a spousal RRSP. You save money if your spouse is in—or will be in—a lower tax bracket when the funds are withdrawn. This is a way to balance incomes at retirement, but you don't have to wait till then. Couples often take cash out of an RRSP to finance a layoff, a parental leave or a sabbatical from work. And as long as the person removing the money is in a low tax bracket, there is little or no tax to pay. (But you will be giving up the benefits of leaving the funds to grow tax-free in the RRSP.)

Say you earn $70,000, you don't have a company pension and your RRSP limit is $12,500. Instead of contributing to your own RRSP, you can contribute to an RRSP for your spouse.

(You get the same tax deduction, whether the money goes into your own or your spouse's RRSP.) Although the funds came from you, your spouse pays the tax on withdrawal—as long as you don't make any spousal contributions in the same year or the two previous years.

Here's an example of how the attribution rules work. It comes from the *Canadian Personal Tax Planning Guide* by KPMG Peat Marwick Thorne. On December 31, 1994, you contribute $12,500 to an RRSP for your spouse for the 1994 tax year. Any withdrawals up to $12,500 from your spouse's RRSP in 1995 or 1996 will be attributed back to you. But on January 1, 1997, your spouse can withdraw the full $12,500 and have the money taxed in his or her hands—provided you made no further spousal RRSP contributions in 1995, 1996 or 1997.

Using the same example, if you contributed for 1994 on January 1, 1995 (rather than on or before December 31, 1994), your spouse would have to wait until January 1, 1998, to withdraw the funds without attribution back to you. For this reason, contributions to a spousal RRSP should not be put off to January or February, as people often do with their own contributions.

You can avoid worrying about these complicated rules if you are the one who will be in a lower tax bracket in the near future. Say you are earning a high income this year but you suspect your job will disappear. Put money in a spousal RRSP this year, and when your spouse removes it next year, it will be taxed in your hands. Since you are unemployed, you may be in a lower tax bracket than your spouse is.

Financial planner Janet Freedman warns that financial institutions routinely make mistakes with spousal RRSPs. Make sure to review the documents to see that the money really is going into a separate plan. And check to see that you have designated your spouse as beneficiary of the RRSP after you die. Don't let the institution write in your estate as beneficiary. This means delays and higher probate costs.

Other Ways to Split Income

If you and your spouse are both over 60 years old, have the higher-income earner apply to share Canada Pension Plan payments with the lower-income spouse. (Quebec Pension Plan payments can also be split, starting in 1994.) The higher earner will pay less tax and may also escape the clawback on Old Age Security. OAS is paid to everyone over 65, but recipients have to start repaying their benefits once their net income tops $53,215.

Finally, there are tax savings that sound piddly but can add up over time. Suppose you have $10,000 to invest outside an RRSP and you can earn an interest rate of 8 per cent. If you give this money to your spouse to invest, the $800 interest is attributed back to you. But if your spouse reinvests that $800 and it generates a further $64 in interest, this "second-generation income" is taxed in your spouse's hands. This income-splitting tactic works well over a long period, but remember to keep accurate records, and perhaps a separate bank account, to separate the two income streams.

Another strategy is to lend, rather than give, money to your spouse to invest in stocks, bonds, gold or real estate. As long as he or she pays interest on the loan at the going rate, the attribution rules don't apply and any money made on the investment is taxed in your spouse's hands. But you will have to report the interest income received from your spouse and pay tax on it, so you won't be much further ahead. The investment has to produce a return well in excess of the loan rate—and this may be hard to achieve.

Getting the Most from Company Benefits

If you work for a medium-sized or large company, you probably get valuable benefits along with your salary. Do you know exactly what your benefits package includes? Can you opt for some benefits and not others? If your employer offers a flexible benefits plan, it's important to make the right choices. You have to co-ordinate your company benefits with the insurance and investments you own outside the workplace, and with your spouse's benefits.

If you are self-employed, you can often piggyback on your partner's benefits. Buying your own coverage can be costly. If both of you are self-employed (perhaps you work together in your own business), you have to decide which benefits are most important to you and look at a package designed for the self-employed.

Health Insurance

If you are married, your spouse is usually covered under your employer's benefit plan for things like dental care, semi-private hospital rooms and prescription drugs. Whether a common-law spouse is covered depends on the employer. Once the Canadian tax law started treating common-law couples in the same way as married couples, many employers updated their benefits too.

As for same-sex spouses, some employers extend benefits to them but many do not. According to *Globe and Mail* workplace reporter Margot Gibb-Clark, a few "seem to be turning a blind eye and offering same-sex benefits informally by just not being too rigorous when an employee fills in forms regarding his or her spouse."

Organizations offering same-sex benefits tend to be large or in the public sector, and the benefits usually apply to medical and dental coverage, but not to pensions. Income tax regulations do not allow registered pension plans to cover couples of the same sex. Until the federal law is changed, employers can offer same-sex survivor pension benefits only by using an unregistered—and less tax-effective—vehicle. They have to set up a separate pension plan for employees with same-sex partners.

Don't forget that the premiums you pay for health and dental insurance, even if they are made by payroll deduction, can be lumped together and claimed as medical expenses for income tax purposes. One spouse can claim the other's medical expenses. If you make a claim, say for a dental appointment or a prescription drug, the deductible amount (what the company doesn't pay) can be claimed as a medical expense.

One of the most common employee perks is life insurance. Most employers pick up the tab for a basic amount—say, one to two times your salary—and offer the chance to buy more coverage at a low group rate. If you are married and you have no children or other dependents, the bare minimum is probably all you need.

But if you and your spouse have a lavish lifestyle, big debts and spend every penny you earn, you should bump up the life insurance coverage to at least five times your income if you can. Before signing up for more group life insurance, compare your company's rates with term insurance you can buy on your own to see which is the better deal. Since there is little job security at any level, it makes sense to diversify your life insurance sources.

When it comes to disability insurance, the same advice applies. If your household depends on your income to meet living expenses, you'll need a disability policy that will replace at least 60 per cent of your income if you are ill or injured and unable to work. Even if you have a group disability plan, topping it up with a private plan will ensure continuity of coverage if you are laid off. Also, you will get better benefits. If your employer allows you to opt out of the group plan, you can buy a private plan and pay the premiums yourself with after-tax dollars. That way, any benefits you collect when you're disabled will be tax-free.

With all your health benefits—drug, dental, optical, hospital and out-of-country medical—check your employee brochures and pay stubs to see how much coverage you get and how much it costs. Don't forget to include your employer's contributions and any deductibles you pay. Then, do the same for your spouse's health benefits. If you are covered under both plans, pick the best or cheapest plan and opt out (if you can) from the inferior one. Why pay for duplicate coverage?

If you are self-employed, adequate disability insurance is a must. Your business could collapse if you are unable to work for an extended period. Disability coverage is expensive, especially when you pay the whole tab, but should be a priority. Life insurance is also important if you have dependents to protect or your partner depends on your income, but dental and health benefits are more a luxury than a necessity.

Retirement Pension Plans

If you have an employer pension plan, you are probably locked into participating. You can't opt out unless you have a group RRSP. Many companies are switching to group RRSPs because they are easier to administer and not as regulated as pension plans. Employees prefer them too because they can understand them. Unless you are a benefits expert, it's extremely difficult to figure out how much your pension plan is worth. Most people don't even know how much their employer is contributing and what rate of return the plan is earning.

Besides being more user-friendly, group RRSPs have other advantages. If you have a cash crunch, you can take out RRSP funds before retirement. Some tax is deducted at source and you may have to pay more when filing your annual tax return, but at least the money is accessible. With a pension plan, the money is locked in until you reach retirement age, even if you leave the company. And most group RRSPs offer members a choice of investments—unlike most pension plans, which give you no say in how the money is invested.

There are two kinds of pension plans and you should know which kind you have. The more common is a defined benefit plan, which guarantees a specific benefit at retirement. The formula is usually based on years of service and earnings.

Actuaries calculate how much the employer and employees will have to contribute to finance the promised benefit.

With a defined benefit plan, you know in advance what your pension will be as a percentage of your earnings. This helps you plan for retirement. The disadvantage is that benefits are generally poor if you leavc the company in mid-career rather than sticking around until retirement. Today, few employees stay with the same employer for their whole working lives.

Less common but increasingly popular is a defined contribution plan, also called a money purchase plan. The employer (and sometimes the employee as well) makes a contribution each year to the plan based on earnings. Typically, contributions equal 5 per cent of annual salary. When you retire, the funds built up in your plan are used to buy an annuity, which provides you with a steady stream of retirement income.

With a defined contribution plan, you don't know in advance how much you will receive. The final amount depends not only on your contributions but also on the plan's earnings and the level of interest rates at retirement. If interest rates are low when you leave the company, you may get a lower retirement income than someone who leaves when rates have risen again. The employer is off the hook and the risk is on your shoulders. The advantage goes to short-term employees and those who leave the company, as they get better benefits than they would under a defined benefit plan.

The type of plan that is better for you depends on your circumstances. If you are job-hopping or planning to take time out from the work force, a defined contribution plan is more advantageous. A defined benefit plan suits people with long years of service at a company, employees over the age of 45 and those hired in mid-career who are near the peak of their earnings, because the pension is based on your years of service and a percentage of your best earnings.

If you are self-employed and have an unincorporated business, contributing to an RRSP will be your only way to build retirement savings. Your net income from the business (after expenses) is considered to be earned income for determining an RRSP contribution limit. If you incorporate your business, you can establish an individual pension plan or IPP, which can be tailored to meet your own circumstances. But IPPs are feasible only if your income is in the $80,000 a year range and growing at least as quickly as the average industrial wage. Deciding whether or not to incorporate is complex, and the chance to set up an IPP is only one factor to consider.

Joint and Survivor Pensions

All pension plans, whether defined contribution or defined benefit, provide a joint and survivor pension to protect your spouse. In fact, unless you opt to take another form of pension, you are usually given a 60 per cent joint and survivor pension. Some provinces give more and others less. This is a minimum standard only. Many company plans provide 75 to 100 per cent of the retiree's benefit to a surviving spouse.

The spouse is not necessarily your legal wife or husband. A spouse is normally defined in the same way as in the province's family law statute. Your common-law partner may have your pension rights and your legal spouse may be excluded.

If you don't want the joint and survivor pension, you can choose another option in most provinces. But as extra protection, your spouse has to agree in writing, usually on a special witnessed form, to waive the coverage. So before you retire, you and your spouse will be faced with this important decision.

Here's an example of how the joint and survivor pension works. (It comes from the Canadian edition of the booklet "Your Pension and Your Spouse", by R. George Martorana and Susan Rowland.) Suppose you and your spouse are both

65 and your company's regular pension is $400 a month. If you select the 60 per cent joint and survivor pension, your regular pension is reduced by a certain amount. The percentage reduction varies from plan to plan and depends on your age and your spouse's age at retirement. Say your pension is reduced by 12 per cent. Then you get $352 a month, instead of $400. If you die first, your spouse receives 60 per cent of the reduced pension—or $211.20 a month—until his or her death.

And what if your spouse dies before you do? How much you get depends on what kind of joint and survivor pension you have. There are two different kinds and most Canadian provinces allow either one to be offered to a retiree. In the first kind, you continue to get $352 a month for the rest of your life, even if your spouse dies first. In the second, once one member of the couple dies, the pension is further reduced so that only the survivor's pension of $211.20 a month is paid—even though you, the retiree, are the survivor.

To decide whether to take the joint and survivor pension, you have to ask yourself some questions. Do you have enough income-producing assets to protect your spouse, even without the pension? Can you buy life insurance to provide additional protection in a different way?

Insurance agents aggressively target people who are about to retire, talking up a strategy to "maximize" your pension. They advise you to choose the single-life option under the company pension plan, which will give you higher income during your life, and ignore the joint and survivor option. They suggest that you use the money you gained by taking the single-life option to buy an insurance policy on your life with your spouse as beneficiary. That will replace the pension for your spouse.

It sounds enticing, but a number of financial consultants say pension maximization is a dangerous area, fraught with potential problems. For one thing, the difference in pension payouts isn't usually large enough to pay for an insurance policy that will adequately protect your spouse. The insurance premium has to cover such items as the agent's commission and the company's overhead and profit. Buying a reasonable amount of life insurance will probably be more costly than the joint and survivor pension.

A life insurance policy also carries interest-rate risk. Most pension max strategies use universal life—a combination of term insurance and an investment account—or interest-sensitive whole life policies. Insurance projections often use high interest rates when estimating premiums and benefits. If interest rates fall, you either have to pay higher premiums to get the same death benefit or you end up with a smaller death benefit.

There's interest-rate risk too when your spouse receives the lump sum from the death benefit. If rates are low, he or she will have limited opportunities to invest the money safely to receive a regular income. With a pension, which has a fixed payout, you don't have that risk. And many company pensions are either indexed for inflation or boosted periodically to keep pace with cost-of-living increases. By replacing a pension with life insurance, you forgo these adjustments.

There is one major advantage with life insurance. If your spouse dies first, you can stop paying the premiums or change the beneficiary. You aren't stuck with a reduced pension payout for life. But the average person is probably better off taking the reduced joint pension and not worrying about it.

The decision to replace a pension with life insurance is complex and requires independent advice. If you are not sure what to do, find a financial advisor who isn't trying to sell life insurance. "Otherwise," says a retirement consultant quoted in the *Wall Street Journal*, "it's like going to a barber to ask him whether you need a haircut. He always replies: 'You need a little off the top.' "

Wills

Marriage and Remarriage

If you are about to get married or remarried and you already have a will, make sure you update it. Marriage revokes an existing will, so if you don't make a new will after your marriage, you will die intestate. In Ontario, the surviving spouse can save the will by filing a special form with the Office of the Estates Registrar. This means that a will which leaves a substantial bequest to the person who was a common-law spouse but who later married the deceased can be valid. Divorce also affects an existing will, as your ex-spouse will be precluded from taking anything under your will (unless your will indicates otherwise). Once you are divorced, an appointment of your ex-spouse as executor of your will is automatically revoked.

If you don't already have a will, you can get one before getting married specifically stating that it is made in contemplation of marriage to a specified person. That way, it is not revoked by marriage to that person. Don't forget, also, to name a new beneficiary on your life insurance policies (including the one at work) and your RRSPs in favour of your new spouse. Neither separation nor divorce will change or revoke a beneficiary designation. (In Quebec, however, divorce does revoke a life insurance beneficiary designation in favour of a spouse.)

Suppose you and your spouse have never been married and do not have any children. Your only major asset is a house, which you own jointly. Do you need a will? Yes. There are several reasons why you should consider getting one done.

- If you have not made a will choosing an executor to handle your affairs, your spouse will not have the immediate power to act on your behalf. He or she will have to apply to the court to be given authority to administer your assets and will have to post a bond, unless a judge orders otherwise. So, there will be less money left in the estate and it will take longer to get into your spouse's hands

- When you die, your spouse inherits the house, and vice versa. But what if you both die together in an accident? If there is no will, the house will be divided 50/50 between each of your estates. Then, it will probably be sold and the proceeds distributed to your respective next of kin, according to the provincial law of intestate succession. If you had a will, you could choose someone to inherit the house if you die together, thus avoiding a forced sale.
- Suppose you and your spouse are in a car crash in which you die immediately and your spouse survives you by a couple of hours. Under the law of intestacy, your spouse's parents and siblings will get everything, while your whole family is disinherited.
- If you have a marriage contract, you can reinforce it with a will that imposes the same financial obligations on your spouse's estate. For example, a husband may be required to support a wife for a specific period, even if he dies during that time. A marriage contract usually has a clause saying it is binding on your heirs, executors and administrators, but contracts can disappear. You have more protection if your spouse's will restates the financial obligations that survive his or her death.

Suppose you have children from previous unions. It is important to have a will that safeguards their interests. If you die intestate, your new spouse (and eventually his or her children) will inherit the bulk of your estate. Legally, you do not have to provide for your children once they become adults, but they can apply to the court for relief if they have been dispossessed by your will and you have supported them financially up to the time of your death.

For those who own a business, it's even more important to protect your spouse and your company with an up-to-date will. A will often goes together with a buy-sell agreement, entitling (and usually requiring) your partners to buy out your shares from your estate at a predetermined price. If there is no buy-sell agreement, your spouse (if named as beneficiary) would have to assume your position in the company, a job he or she may not be qualified for or interested in assuming.

Business owners should also cover their debts. Since debts must be paid out of an estate before any money is distributed to heirs, you should have enough liquid assets or life insurance to pay off outstanding bank loans, lines of credit or mortgages registered against your home. Life insurance can also be used to provide cash for your partners to buy out your interest.

Common-Law and Same-Sex Partnerships

If you don't have a cohabitation contract, you definitely need a will if you want your partner to inherit from you when you die. Under intestacy laws, there is no legal protection for lovers, friends and companions. If you were married before and you never got a divorce, make sure you changed your will on separation. Your separation agreement should release you from claims by your spouse against your estate.

An added complication arises if one partner has a terminal illness—such as cancer or AIDS—and makes or amends a will naming the other as beneficiary shortly before death. The family can challenge the will in court, saying it was prepared under duress or while the person was not of sound mind. This has happened a number of times in Canada. Unmarried and same-sex couples should make out their wills early to avoid such clashes. And if they are sick at the time of making the will, they should have a doctor certify that they are in a competent mental state.

In one recent case, the elderly parents of a man who died from AIDS contested his will, which left his house to his same-sex partner. They argued that they had a right to the house after giving their son a loan of more than $60,000 to pay off the mortgage, on the condition that the house be left to them or their other son. But the man's lawyer successfully argued that the parents gave the money with no strings attached. The law assumes that money given from parents to children is a gift unless the parents can prove otherwise.

In other cases, parents have come into the picture at the last minute, persuading a terminally ill same-sex partner to change the will and give everything to the family. The parents fight for the life insurance too. If you are in this position, hold your ground and put everything in writing.

Some couples may want to consider ways to transfer property to one another outside of a will. If a member of the deceased's biological family is going to challenge the surviving partner's right to inherit, the will is the likely arena. One way to avoid a legal fight is to register shared property, such as a house or a bank account, in both names as "joint tenants with right of survivorship." When one partner dies, the property belongs to the survivor. Do this early on, as a change in ownership while terminally ill could open the door to challenges based on a lack of mental capacity.

The key to success in a relationship is being open with each other—and that includes sharing your feelings and fears about money. By establishing the lines of communication early, you may be able to keep your love alive and your union intact for a lifetime. But if, for whatever reasons, you can no longer stay together, your openness about money and your advance arrangements should make it easier for you to split up. Couples who have negotiated a domestic contract sometimes find there is nothing to fight about when they divorce. Everything has been decided ahead of time.

2 SEPARATION, DIVORCE AND REMARRIAGE

You may think this chapter has no relevance if you are happily married or living in a stable relationship. No one wants to plan for a divorce. But everyone should be aware of the financial consequences of breaking up, in case it happens to you or someone close to you. Almost three in ten Canadian marriages do not last. Yet divorce does not seem to erode people's faith in the institution of marriage, since seven out of ten divorced Canadians remarry.

Edward and I recently celebrated our twentieth anniversary. An event once considered commonplace for couples now elicited amazement from people we knew. "I can't believe someone I know has been married 20 years," one friend blurted out. "I thought only my parents' generation did that." Indeed, Edward and I have seen marital strife and nasty splits among our friends and associates—and we can imagine how debilitating the breakdown of a close relationship can be.

At a time of great personal anguish and uncertainty, you and your partner will have to make some important financial decisions. What is a fair level of spousal and child support? How do you disentangle your joint accounts and establish credit on your own? Is it possible to split your pensions and retirement savings plans? The lawyer handling your divorce will bring these issues to your attention but may not be qualified to give in-depth advice on personal finance. In the throes of a separation, it is wise to seek the services of a financial planner as well.

You can find help through your workplace (especially if your company has an employee assistance program), your municipal social services branch or the Canadian Association of Financial Planners, a national organization based in Toronto. Ask all the advisors you interview if they are paid only for advice or if they earn commissions by selling you products such as insurance or mutual funds.

What to Do Before You Split Up

Divorce does not affect both partners equally. Women and children often find themselves living in poverty after separation and divorce, whereas men's disposable income usually goes up. Most court-ordered support payments are in arrears—and even among those who do receive support, two-thirds have incomes below the poverty line. Children of poor families tend to have more health problems, fare worse at school and develop more behavioural problems than other children. The growing number of families headed by single mothers is a real social concern.

If you are a woman, you have to recognize the harsh financial facts. "The cold truth is that your husband probably earns quite a bit more than you do," say Betsy Matthews and Richard Birch, a husband-and-wife writer team, in *Taking Care of Tomorrow: The Canadian Money Book for Prime Time Women*. "If your children are still at home, you will have most of the responsibility of raising them and you'll bear most of the cost. And your ex-husband will not come through with much, or any, of the money he promised or which he owes according to the court order that came with your divorce." (Fortunately, some provinces such as Ontario have stepped up their enforcement of child support from "deadbeat dads" by garnishing their wages.)

This doesn't mean you shouldn't try to get the best settlement you can from your ex. But you must realize there's a very strong chance, especially if you're a woman, that you won't continue to enjoy the same standard of living as before—at least temporarily if not permanently. It costs a lot more for your ex to maintain two households than one.

If your marriage seems shaky, try to get a handle on your finances. Your lawyer will demand a great deal of documentation, such as records and receipts, to negotiate the financial aspects of your separation agreement and divorce settlement. Make sure you have detailed estimates of what it costs to maintain your household and your spouse's ability to pay.

Collect information on all household expenditures in the last year or two. This will give you a clearer idea of what you will need to live on in the future. Include any anticipated costs, such as eyeglasses or orthodontia, monthly payments on a new car, furnace, roof and so on. Go through bank statements and credit card bills to put together a detailed picture.

Then, figure out roughly what the other partner's income and expenses will be, so you can negotiate a realistic and fair support payment. The best time to complete this accounting is before you actually separate, while the family's financial records are still available to both spouses. If your partner has always looked after the household expenses, this is a good opportunity to get acquainted with them.

Other Ways to Protect Yourself Before a Separation

Make sure you are listed as the primary driver on the family car insurance policy. If your name appears as the secondary driver and your spouse cancels the policy, you could be forced to get a new policy at a beginner's higher rate.

Since joint bank accounts can be closed and joint credit cards cancelled, establish your own banking and credit identity. Open a separate bank account if you don't already have one, and start putting your wages and other money into it. Get a loan or credit card in your own name and pay it off religiously. Make sure your credit record is separate from your spouse's by calling your local credit bureau and asking to see your file. If you don't have a credit history, get to work immediately to establish one.

Many financial institutions offer secured Visa and MasterCards to borrowers who have never had credit or who are normally considered poor risks. To get a secured card, you have to deposit money that is at least equal to the credit line you want to receive. Check several banks to find the lowest deposit requirement. After maintaining your account properly for a year or so, you may qualify for a standard card and get back your deposit with interest.

Know what mortgages or loans—either personal or business—you have co-signed with your spouse and try to keep funds aside in case you have to cover the payments. If your spouse defaults, you may be harassed by collection agencies or money may be deducted from your paycheque or bank account. Once you have separated, consider giving notice to the financial institution that you are revoking your loan guarantee. This will let you off the hook for debts incurred in the future, but not for past debts.

If you can't cope financially and you are in debt over your head, consult a non-profit or government-operated credit counselling service. It will set a realistic budget for you and arrange with your creditors to halt further interest payments, reduce your debt or pay it back more slowly. If there is no such resource in your community, talk to a bankruptcy trustee about making a voluntary proposal to your creditors. You will pay a fee to the trustee (and maybe to the credit counsellor) for administering your plan.

Bankruptcy should be a last resort. Don't file for personal bankruptcy without the advice and encouragement of your lawyer, warns *The Canadian Divorce Decisions Workbook*: "Financial problems during a divorce can seem overwhelming but may have an eventual solution without seriously marring your credit."

Separating from Your Spouse

The Need for a Lawyer

Once your marriage has broken down, seek out a lawyer as soon as possible. You have a lot of difficult work ahead of you: to buy or sell the family home, divide other assets, review life insurance policies, take out or update a will and calculate support payments. Don't try to cut costs by hiring a less experienced lawyer. Good legal advice will cost a bundle but will save you money in the long run, and in some cases, the fees are tax-deductible.

(The rules for deducting legal fees are tricky, so consult a tax expert before you make a claim. Legal expenses are deductible if you are suing your spouse to *enforce* support granted in a separation agreement or by court order, but not if you are trying to *establish* the right to support. Get an itemized statement from your lawyer, so you can claim any tax deductions to which you're entitled.)

Every province has a form of legal aid for people who cannot afford legal services. You have to apply, proving financial need, before you can be accepted.

Ask your family lawyer for referrals or talk to divorced friends who feel that, on balance, their experience was good. "If they start frothing about how poorly they were represented, ask for the name of their spouse's lawyer," advises *Fortune* magazine. Most lawyers ask for an up-front retainer when they accept your case, but make sure it's refundable if you and your spouse reconcile shortly afterward.

How much will you pay? It's hard to estimate the total amount, since a lawyer can't tell in advance how long the negotiations will take. Nevertheless, ask for a written contract or retainer form that spells out the hourly rate that will be charged.

Don't hesitate to ask the lawyer to put a ceiling, or upper limit, on the fee that can be charged without further written authorization, says lawyer Michael Cochrane in *Surviving Divorce: The Everyday Guide to Canadian Family Law*. Also, insist on a specific description of the work—a simple "Obtain divorce" is the equivalent of a blank cheque—and authorize only the first few steps. This will stop the lawyer from litigating first and negotiating later, and give you more control over the work.

Divorce Mediation

Not all couples can work out their differences in mediation, but if you are able to, mediation can be a less expensive, less combative alternative to the conventional legal system. Unlike the adversarial courtroom approach, mediation uses a skilled third party to help couples discuss issues such as custody, access or division of assets and come up with a mutually satisfactory solution. "It has the potential to be the most important development in family law in decades," says Mr. Cochrane.

The mediator isn't on either spouse's side, but tries to help both of you discuss your needs in a rational, less emotionally charged way. Mediation usually isn't binding. A final agreement must still be written up by lawyers for each spouse.

Under the federal Divorce Act of 1985, lawyers have a duty to inform clients about mediation facilities that can help them negotiate a settlement. But if your lawyer forgets to tell you, check with family therapists and mental health agencies to get names of mediators in your area. In interviews, ask for references from lawyers and clients and check the person's educational credentials and training.

Financial Support

When your marriage ends, you and your children are entitled to receive financial support from your ex-spouse if your circumstances warrant it. Spousal support is usually short-term, lasting only until you become economically self-sufficient. But support payments for children can go on for years. The legal definition of when a parent's financial responsibility to a child ends is at age sixteen, but this can be extended to university graduation.

You can also get financial support after leaving a common-law relationship. Seven out of ten Canadian provinces have laws that establish support rights between unmarried spouses of the opposite sex. (There are no corresponding rights for same-sex couples.) The couple must have lived together for a certain minimum period, ranging from one to five years, except if they have a child together. And there must be a marriage-like relationship, which implies shared household responsibilities and expenses, plus some degree of stability and commitment.

Spousal support is rare for unmarried couples who are childless, note Julien and Marilyn Payne, a team of family law consultants, in their book, *Dealing with Family Law: A Canadian Guide*. This is because the partners are usually free to find gainful employment and pay their own way.

Child support is always legally available from the parents, whether they are married or not. "A child's needs are not dependent on whether his or her parents are married," the Paynes say, "and both parents must contribute to the child's support in accordance with their ability to pay."

Taxability of Support Payments

In the fall of 1994, Suzanne Thibaudeau of Trois-Rivières, Quebec, took her case before the Supreme Court of Canada to argue that she and other custodial parents were being discriminated against by having to pay income tax on child support payments from an ex-spouse. She was successful at the

Federal Court of Appeal, but the federal government launched an appeal. The Supreme Court heard the appeal but has reserved judgment. Until there is a final decision, parents in similar circumstances have to pay the tax. But they can file a "notice of objection" to ensure their returns are reassessed based on the outcome of the case.

Under the current rules, alimony and maintenance payments (including spousal and child support) are tax-deductible to the payer and taxable to the recipient if they meet the following conditions:

- The payments must be periodic, rather than a one-time lump sum. Lump sum payments, which are less frequently awarded to separating spouses, are tax-neutral. The payer does not get a tax deduction and the recipient does not pay tax on the money received.
- The payments must be made pursuant to a court order or written agreement. If the payer gives more than is called for, say for gifts or pocket money for the children, the extra amount is not tax-deductible to the payer or taxable to the recipient.
- The spouses must be living apart from each other, by virtue of a breakdown of the marital relationship, at the time the payments are made and throughout the remainder of the year. If they reconcile during any year, the payer loses the ability to deduct support payments for the tax year.
- The payments must be in the form of an allowance, meaning that the recipient has complete control over how they are used and does not have to account for them.

When negotiating support, the tax consequences should be a major consideration for you and your lawyer. Suppose your spouse agrees to give you $300 a month to raise your children. That $3,600 is included in your income for the year and you have to pay tax on it. So you should ask for a higher amount, say $400 a month, to pay the tax bill and end up with $300 in your pocket. If the tax is impossible to calculate in advance, your spouse can make a taxable payment to you later on to cover the tax owing.

Unfortunately, tax implications are not always taken into account when determining support payments. The non-custodial parent—usually the father—may not earn enough to pay an added amount to cover the taxes. He pays what he can, but the wife still has to pay income tax on what she gets. Sometimes, the husband will not agree in a negotiated settlement to pay more child support to cover the taxes, and the wife chooses not to fight it, or cannot afford to fight it.

When the income tax rule was enacted in 1942, most support payers were men and were in a higher tax bracket than their ex-wives, who usually stayed home. The government wanted to give men an incentive to pay and even increase their support payments. But it has not worked out that way. Many support payers just pocket the tax savings, rather than passing them on to their families. And many single mothers are in the work force, often in the same tax bracket as their former spouses.

If the Thibaudeau case stands up in the Supreme Court, custodial parents may be no better off. Non-custodial parents will rush to court to ask for a reduction in their child support, claiming the amount was set too high because it was based on being taxable to the recipient and deductible to the payer. But win or lose, the protesters have a bigger goal. They want Canada to adopt the model used in the United States and other countries, where child support payments are neither tax-deductible to the payer nor taxable to the recipient.

If you are receiving periodic spousal or child support payments, make sure you set enough money aside during the year to pay the tax bill. If you have a full-time job, ask your employer to increase the amount of income tax deducted at source. This will prevent the hardship of having to write a big cheque to Revenue Canada when filing your annual tax return. And if you are a non-custodial parent who is paying support, you can get tax relief by contacting the district office of Revenue Canada. It will tell your employer to reduce the amount of income tax withheld from your pay.

One consolation of taxable support payments is that they count as earned income for RRSPs. So, a custodial parent receiving child support will usually have a higher RRSP contribution limit. Conversely, payers of tax-deductible support may have less RRSP contribution room.

Ensuring Support Payments

If you are receiving child support, you want to ensure the payments will continue if your spouse dies suddenly or becomes disabled. Your lawyer, when drafting the separation agreement, will probably insert a clause requiring the support payer to buy and maintain life and disability insurance. You should be named as irrevocable beneficiary of these policies so your spouse can't remove you as beneficiary without your consent or, if there is a cash value built up, cancel the policy to gain access to that value.

However, even if you are not named as irrevocable beneficiary, your spouse can neglect to pay the premiums on the insurance policies so they lapse. Irrevocable designation has nothing to do with a guarantee of premium payment. For guaranteed protection, you should own the policy on your spouse's life and pay the premiums yourself. This can be a negotiating point for higher support payments, or you can later go to court to recover the payments.

If you are the one who is paying support, you might want to set up an insurance trust in your will. After you die, the insurance benefits would be paid into the trust and the trustees would make support payments as long as they are required. Once your legal obligations are fulfilled, the rest of the money would go to another person you would name. This gives you more flexibility and ensures the insurance benefits won't go into your estate, where they could be seized to pay creditors.

If you named your spouse as beneficiary under any life insurance policies (both individual and group)—or RRSPs, RRIFs, annuities or pension plans—then review these designations and name new beneficiaries. Neither separation nor divorce will revoke beneficiary designations (except in Quebec). Some insurance contracts have an irrevocable designation, which you cannot change without the beneficiary's consent. This consent could be tricky to get.

Wills

Give immediate attention to revising your will when your marriage breaks down. Divorce revokes any gifts (such as items of value) or monetary bequests made to a former spouse, but separation does not. Make sure you are not leaving anything to your spouse that you do not want him or her to have. And if you named your spouse as an executor of your estate, choose someone else.

If you have no will, get one drafted post-haste. The reason is that provincial intestacy laws guarantee your spouse a large chunk of your assets if you are still legally married. If you have no children, your former flame could end up with everything.

Another question that comes up with wills is what happens to spousal or child support obligations if the payer dies. Does the estate have to continue the payments? Several provinces have laws ensuring that support will be paid by the payer's estate. (Incidentally, support payments made in the year of the payer's death or any later tax year are *not* taxable to the recipient or deductible to the estate.) If you are leaving cash bequests to a spouse and child, you should specify in your will whether these gifts are in addition to the support obligation or meant to replace it.

Other Ways to Protect Yourself After a Separation

These precautions to take to protect yourself financially are courtesy of Toronto law firm Torkin Manes Cohen & Arbus:

- If you own any real estate in joint tenancy with a spouse, change the ownership to a tenancy in common.
- Remove your spouse as signing authority on personal bank accounts. Cancel your spouse's right to have access to your safety-deposit box.
- Revoke any power of attorney you may have given to your spouse. Deliver the written revocation to him or her and demand the return of all executed copies.
- Reconsider your estate plan. Remember, there will be tax to pay when you leave appreciated property or RRSPs to someone other than your spouse. Tax is deferred with transfers between spouses. As a result, you may have to increase your life insurance coverage to deal with any significant tax bite that arises after your death, since you are giving up those tax deferrals.

Dividing the Family's Property

When a marriage breaks down, the division of family property is governed by provincial law. It's hard to generalize, because each province has its own arrangement. Some provinces still distinguish between "family assets"—those shared equally at divorce—and other assets that are, as a rule, not shared.

Ontario has the most radical scheme. Under the Family Law Act introduced in 1986, the increase in value of all property acquired during the marriage, irrespective of ownership, is equally divided when the marriage breaks down. (There are a few exceptions, such as inheritances received during the marriage—unless the money was invested in the family home.) Lawyers for each spouse do two net worth statements, one at the date of marriage, another at the date of separation. If one spouse's net worth increase during the relationship is greater than the other spouse's net worth increase during that period, the courts will order one spouse to make an equalization payment to the other. This can be done through a cash payment or, if cash is not available, through a transfer of property.

You can avoid this 50/50 property sharing by having a marriage contract that exempts certain assets from division. Marriage contracts are fairly common among small business owners and partners who have been married before. But many couples shy away from them, finding it unromantic to negotiate property division when they don't intend to break up.

However, there are some rights you cannot sign away in a marriage contract. Every province puts restrictions on one spouse's ability to sell or mortgage the family home without the other's consent. This protects the value of the property for possession if the marriage breaks down.

The Family Home

In any separation, a major question is what happens to the family home. This is the most valuable asset for many couples and, if one spouse decides to stay in the home, he or she must pay off the other. The problem is, how do you come up with enough cash to buy out your partner without having to arrange a large mortgage? Sometimes, though this is not the outcome you want, you may be forced to sell the home, split any cash proceeds with your spouse and start over again.

Couples can choose to swap assets. For example, if a husband owes his wife $100,000 to buy out her share of the house, he can give her other assets, such as his RRSP. Under the Income Tax Act, you can do a tax-free rollover of your

RRSPs to your spouse's RRSP as long as the two of you are living apart and the transfer is made under the terms of a written separation agreement or court order as a property settlement. (You can't do it as a support obligation on a tax-free basis.)

RRSPs are attractive to spouses who do not need the funds for a long time, but may not be suitable if you need cash up front. If you have to collapse the RRSP, you will pay tax on all the money you receive. If you are withdrawing money from a spousal RRSP after separation, the usual three-year attribution rule does not apply. The money is taxed in your hands, even if your spouse was the sole contributor.

Falling real estate prices can create a problem, especially in those provinces (Ontario being one example) where the value of a couple's assets is set at the date of separation. In that case, one spouse often has to give the other far more than a house is worth by the time the property settlement is to be made. The general rule is that the spouse in whose name the asset is registered bears the consequences if the asset goes up or down in value between the separation date and the date of settlement.

For example, say the family home is worth $300,000 when a couple separates, and the wife agrees to buy out her husband's share for $150,000. The settlement takes a year to finalize, and by that time the house's value has dropped to $250,000. If the house is registered in the wife's name, she alone suffers. She still has to pay her husband $150,000 and he pockets the windfall profit of $25,000.

Of course, this scenario works to the wife's benefit if the house goes up to $400,000 in the same period. She buys out her husband's share for $150,000, less than half the current value, and gets to keep $250,000 if she decides to sell the house right away. This problem often leads the "losing" spouse to argue for a court finding of a constructive trust, whereby the other spouse must share the profit or loss as a result of the change in value from the date of separation to the date of judgment.

Pension Plans

After the family home, a pension is often a couple's most valuable asset; if you have a company pension plan, your spouse may be entitled to a share of it. But deciding how to divide pensions after separation has kept an army of lawyers and actuaries busy for the last decade. How exactly do you determine the value of a pension that won't be paid for many years? How do you factor in early retirement benefits and inflation indexing?

Be prepared for long and difficult negotiations over the value of a pension. If your lawyer wants to hire a professional valuator to settle these questions, remember that bills for valuations will be costly and will be passed on to you. "It is important that you receive an estimate from your lawyer in advance before authorizing the valuation of an asset as significant as a pension," Mr. Cochrane says in his family law guide.

Since pensions can be hard to split, spouses often agree to swap a pension against another asset in the divorce settlement—if this is possible. You may be able to strike a deal where you keep the full pension and your spouse gets your interest in the family home—or vice versa. However, every province treats pensions somewhat differently. In Manitoba, for example, the pension accumulated during the marriage must be divided 50/50; divorcing spouses can't trade off pensions against other assets.

Canada Pension Plan or Quebec Pension Plan benefits can be shared after separation or divorce, or at the end of a common-law relationship. One spouse might give the other spouse half of the pension credits accumulated during the years of the marriage. This will ensure that a non-working wife who was not eligible to contribute to CPP/QPP during the marriage ends up with some pension coverage. If both spouses had roughly the same incomes while they were married, their pension credits won't change.

Your lawyer will handle the CPP/QPP pension-splitting for you, or you can do it yourself by getting an application at a local Canada Pension Plan office (part of the new federal Department of Human Resources). Your spouse's CPP/QPP credits will be transferred to your account; if you don't have an account, one will be opened for you. You can start receiving a reduced pension at age 60 if you have substantially stopped working, or you can wait till you qualify for a full pension at age 65.

Life as a Single Parent

When children and money are involved, the first marriage never ends—even when both partners remarry. There are still financial and emotional ties to the past. But if you and your ex-spouse are constructive in working with your children during and after divorce, you can all come through "family surgery" without too many scars.

You will face a number of lifestyle adjustments as you split one household into two. Both partners may have to find a new place to live, each big enough to accommodate children if shared parenting is involved. There will be moving expenses, home renovations and redecoration. A spouse who has stayed home and raised children during the marriage may have to go through career counselling and retraining.

Custody

If there is any post-separation wrangling, it will probably centre on child support and custody/access arrangements. In the past, mothers routinely were given sole custody of the children and fathers paid child support in exchange for reasonable access. But today, many parents are opting for some sort of joint custody arrangement.

In general, joint custody means that both parents share in making major decisions involving their children. There is no statutory definition of this parenting plan in either the provincial legislation or the federal Divorce Act. "Basically, it is whatever people want it to be," says Laurie Coulter, a Toronto writer and co-parent in *Two Homes: A Parent's Guide to Joint Custody in Canada.*

In one form of joint custody, the decision-making is shared but not necessarily the physical care of the children. The children live most of the time with one parent, and the other spends occasional time with the children. Some people don't mind a flexible time-sharing arrangement; others prefer a fixed schedule—for example, one parent has the children every other weekend and one night during the week.

This type of joint custody, without shared physical care, raises two questions for the primary caregiver, says Ms. Coulter. Are you willing to share the decision-making about your children with a former partner who is unable or unwilling to take on a significant share of the day-to-day care? And will you be adequately compensated for that care? "Some lawyers caution that if you call this arrangement joint custody rather than sole custody with liberal access, you may have trouble obtaining an appropriate amount of child support as the custodial parent," she advises.

If the parents agree on joint physical custody, they share the daily care and responsibility for the children. The arrangements are varied and often evolve over time. One divorced couple we know used to split the week, with the children moving from one house to the other each Wednesday and Saturday. As the kids got older, they found it easier to spend alternate weeks with each parent. Another couple we know with teenaged children splits the year, with six months on and six months off.

Shared parenting is tricky and will not work unless the former spouses are highly organized, flexible and committed. Since mutual trust and cooperation are often lacking after a divorce, the courts generally do not order joint custody unless both parents agree to it beforehand. In choosing this plan, you may feel like a pioneer, with no childhood experiences to draw on and few successful role models. But if you have a sincere conviction that joint custody is right for your children, you should be able to live with the complications.

In any case, a court order giving custody to both parents can be changed later if your circumstances change. For example, you or your ex-spouse may move out of town, get married again or become ill. And for whatever reason, some children do not do well in a shared parenting plan. Ms. Coulter cites the case of a three-year-old boy who was not an easy child before the divorce and became uncontrollable afterward. Once the arrangement was changed—the mother was given responsibility for his daily care and the father got plenty of access—the boy's behaviour improved dramatically.

Visitation Rights

When arranging or rearranging child custody arrangements, don't forget your own and your spouse's parents. Studies show that grandparents can be a stabilizing force in the lives of children whose parents have separated. They can offer unconditional love, a sense of security and a unique window on the past. Make sure to include visitation rights for both sets of grandparents. If something happens to you and your spouse gets custody of the kids, you don't want your parents to be shut out.

Most states have enacted laws giving visitation rights to grandparents, no matter who gets custody. In Canada, the Divorce Act allows persons other than the parents (the word "grandparent" is not used) to participate in legal proceedings involving a child. If grandparents get the court's permission to intervene, they can apply for access to the child after divorce. The court will then decide what is in the child's best interests.

Under provincial custody and access laws, lawyer Michael Cochrane says, grandparents can apply for access to grandchildren when a common-law relationship ends. Also, grandparents can apply for access under provincial laws if they are being shut out from their grandchildren's lives for a particular reason, good or bad, when the parents' marriage or common-law union is still intact.

Grandparents should see legal proceedings only as a last resort, Mr. Cochrane says. A better alternative is family counselling and, if possible, the use of mediation to sort out the barriers to contact between children and grandparents. "Do not threaten to sue, to withdraw financial support, to eliminate inheritances, to cut out new partners or to penalize the couple in any way," he advises grandparents. "If you feel strongly about inheritances and other financial relations between yourself and the couple, you are free to make whatever arrangements you wish, but I believe it is a mistake to connect them to spending time with the child."

Support Payments

After divorce, parents may have to change their child support arrangements. Monthly support payments, although usually indexed to inflation, may grow too skimpy as the child gets older. In the preteen and teen years, there are often major expenses such as orthodontic work, car insurance and post-secondary education. Parents should anticipate, and make plans to share, these costs in advance, to avoid time-consuming and expensive legal battles.

If you are paying child support, remember that you will get tax relief only for amounts specified in the separation agreement or court order. Any money you hand over beyond your legal obligation is not tax-deductible. This includes direct payments to the child or a lump-sum payment to the custodial parent.

One single father we know was not aware of this tax wrinkle. For several years, he generously paid more than he had to (his ex-wife said she needed more), then belatedly discovered his extra payments were not tax-deductible. When Revenue Canada finally caught up to him, he owed more than $10,000 in back taxes, plus penalties. It took him several years of scrimping and saving to pay his tax bill. He's more careful now.

Non-custodial parents paying child support can also get relief if the other parent decides to move farther away and has a good reason, such as a better job. In these cases, the courts often order a reduction in the amount of child support paid because of the extra expenses involved in family visits. Lawyer Michael Cochrane mentions a case where a mother moved from Toronto to Calgary and the father's child support payments were lowered by $100 a month to compensate for travel costs he would incur.

The most common source of problems, however, is default by the support payer on his or her obligations. Every province and territory has automatic support and custody enforcement services, which tend to be overused, understaffed and backlogged. But they do provide service free of charge, while lawyers and mediators charge fees for similar enforcement work. In Ontario, courts can order a delinquent spouse's employer to deduct support payments from his or her wages. Since the automatic wage deduction plan went into effect in March 1992, compliance has improved dramatically.

Unfortunately, it's hard to chase a deadbeat parent who moves from one province to another. Though a support order can be registered in the courts of the new province to which the debtor has moved, it is usually difficult to enforce. There is no nationwide support enforcement body in Canada that can garnish a person's wages, bank accounts or income tax refunds owed.

Bankruptcy

Federal bankruptcy laws can also affect your divorce. By filing for bankruptcy, an overcommitted debtor gets a fresh start by wiping out most debts. Spousal and child support obligations survive a bankruptcy, but most other debts are cancelled. This means that obligations intended to carry out the terms of a property settlement—such as lump-sum payments to buy out a share of home ownership—may be cancelled. Your lawyer should keep the prospect of bankruptcy in mind when structuring a settlement.

What Happens If You Die?

As a single parent, it is important for you to ensure that your children are taken care of after you die. The separation agreement may provide for an insurance policy on the support payer's life, but both parents need insurance to cover funeral and estate settlement and long-term expenses such as mortgage payments and university education. Also, disability insurance should be maintained on both the mother and father.

Tax Credits and Deductions for Parents

Taxes will not be high on your list of priorities, but separated parents can often save money by claiming certain credits and deductions. For example, a mother who previously stayed home with the children can deduct a portion of the child care expenses incurred when she goes back to work. Also, single parents who support children can claim the equivalent-to-spouse credit for one of the kids. This was worth $5,380 in 1993.

The equivalent-to-spouse credit, while lucrative, has certain restrictions. Both parents cannot claim it for the same child. It cannot be claimed by a parent who is deducting payments made for that child's support. And if one parent has a common-law spouse, he or she cannot also claim the equivalent-to-spouse amount for a dependent child. There can only be one equivalent-to-spouse credit for each address.

As a single parent, you can ask the government to recalculate the child tax benefit based only on your own income—rather than the combined income for you and your ex-spouse. This will almost always result in a higher benefit to you. Call

1-800-387-1193, or notify your district taxation office or the income security programs office of Human Resources Canada.

Revenue Canada has published a 30-page booklet, "Alimony or Maintenance", that explains the tax law relating to separation and divorce. It's an excellent publication, replete with details and examples of how these often complicated rules work. For a free copy, check with your district taxation office.

Remarriage and Blended Families

In 1990, there were 343,000 blended families in Canada, representing 7 per cent of all families raising children. "It used to be common to ask parents how many children they had. Today, one asks children how many parents they have," says *Profiling Canada's Families*, a publication of the Vanier Institute of the Family. Reconstituting a family and combining children from former relationships is a big step that often requires discussion and counselling. Hence the growth in self-help books, support groups and special therapists or "remarriage counsellors."

Studies have shown that money-related issues wreck remarriages as often as child-related problems, says U.S. family finance writer Patricia Schiff Estess in *Remarriage and Your Money: Once Again for Richer or Poorer.* Couples saying "I do" for the second, third or fourth time often have differing attitudes toward money and ways of managing, earning and spending it. As you get older, your money habits become more entrenched and harder to change, even when they conflict with those of your partner.

Child custody and support arrangements can be thrown into disarray when former spouses enter into new relationships after divorce. Issues that were settled long ago may resurface when a stepparent joins the family, and the old hurtful feelings may return. Both children and ex-spouses need to be reassured that the stepparent is not taking over the parental role.

After going through a divorce, you may be more anxious to draft a prenuptial contract before you remarry. When there are children from a previous marriage, the contract may include references to their financial support. Who pays for private school or university tuition fees—the non-custodial parent or the stepparent? Does a former spouse who is well off pay for the children's orthodontal work if it isn't included in the separation agreement? Should the stepfather buy a car for a teenaged child if the natural father says no?

Often the first order of financial business a remarried couple must address is where to live. Should they hold on to one of their houses or buy a house neither has lived in before? From a psychological standpoint, neutral space is a good way to start a new life together, says Ms. Estess. This assumes that you can afford it and there are no militating factors, such as the need to be near a special school, doctor or instructor, or a separation agreement that prohibits a move until a child reaches a certain age.

When selling a house, it's smart to talk to a tax advisor about maximizing the principal residence exemption. If you and your former spouse owned two homes at the time of marriage breakdown, you can claim only one of them as a principal residence for the years you were married and living together after 1981. This means there may be capital gains tax owing on the sale.

If you decide to stay in a home that one spouse lived in before remarriage—perhaps because you don't want to uproot the children—you should try to exorcize the ghosts of the past that may haunt the old residence. This means shuffling bedrooms, redecorating or replacing some of the furniture. A new spouse might want to assume a mortgage on the house or buy out the former spouse's share. If this is unaffordable, both partners can take out a loan to pay off the former spouse.

Remarried households often have more children living at home and may be worse off economically than other types of families. When there's not enough money, resentment can erupt. Stepfathers often feel drained by the financial obligations of the other spouse, especially when a former husband skips out on support. Stepmothers who are financially independent and bring no children of their own to the new marriage may find themselves contributing to the support of a former wife who refuses to work or can't.

Remarrieds have the same choices as others caught in a fiscal squeeze—they can spend less or earn more. Also, a custodial parent can go after a former partner who is not providing the agreed-upon support. And a parent who is paying support can ask the court to reduce the amount.

To modify your child support payments, you have to prove there has been a substantial change in your financial position, one that was not anticipated when the original payments were set. In general, courts will deny a request for lower child support simply because a non-custodial parent remarries. They hold that earlier obligations come first—an approach that's been called "vasectomy by dollar bill." A husband cannot claim his new obligations are more important than his duty to support his first family, especially if he voluntarily assumes financial responsibility for stepchildren.

New Children

The birth of a child often adds to the financial pressure for remarried couples. In a "yours, mine and ours" family, children from previous relationships are combined with a new child the couple has together. If you and your spouse are thinking of enlarging your brood, start taking financial precautions right away. This means beefing up your emergency fund (in case either parent has to take time off work), updating and increasing your life and disability insurance, and starting an education fund.

You also should revise your wills and name a guardian for the new child, in the event that you both die. This can be a problem if there are other children living in your family, who presumably will be looked after by your former spouse. The younger child will be shunted off to a relative or friend while his or her familiar and well-loved half siblings will go in another direction. "Unless yours is an unusual setup," says Ms. Estess, "siblings will be split."

Another dilemma: How do you divide your estate among children in their teens or twenties and a young child? Can you justify unequal bequests? It may seem unfair, but the baby in the family probably needs more material support than an 18-year-old who has already been supplied with many things. If you do leave different amounts, explain the rationale of your decisions with children old enough to understand, who may feel slighted or resentful about getting less.

One way to get around this apparent inequality is to leave money in a trust for all your children after you die. The trustees should have the power to distribute funds to each child as needed. Eventually, when the younger children are grown and have completed their education, whatever is left can be divided among all the offspring.

Parents have to stay alert to the fact that teenagers sometimes see a new half sibling as a little intruder, putting a hand directly into their pockets, even when that's not the case. Ms. Estess met a 16-year-old boy who thought his mother and stepfather would get him a car because most of his friends' parents did. Then the baby came and they said no. It took countless hours of explaining for the boy to understand that the refusal wasn't linked to the baby. His parents wanted him to wait till he turned 18 and saved some money for the purchase. But with the excitement of the pregnancy and the chaos of establishing a family life, they had never talked about it before.

Still, parents in blended families often have cause to suspect their children are using guilt to try to manipulate them. Kids love to play the fairness issue, complaining that a half-brother or half-sister got something they didn't get. "Even if they are hundreds of miles apart, former families and new families *seem* to know exactly how the other family is living—and it's always extravagantly," says Ms. Estess.

In every family, whether intact or blended, parents have to deal with the question of what to tell children about their finances. But it's more complicated in remarriages, because there are more people involved and most partners aren't anxious to give children sensitive information that may be shared with a former spouse. The decision what to tell and not to tell depends on the age and maturity of the children and how comfortable all the adults feel in discussing the financial facts of life.

In *Remarriage and Your Money,* Ms. Estess gives sensible advice on talking to children in terms they can understand. "Without drawing children into the fray with former spouses," says Ms. Estess, "parents and stepparents have to be able to explain problems as unemotionally as possible in ways that do not make the children feel they are the cause of the plight or responsible for finding the solutions to financial problems. In some cases where the children are old enough to understand, it makes sense to explain, where they're involved, the terms of a separation agreement signed with a former spouse."

For example, a father found his kids were furious with him because their mother told them she wasn't getting any financial support. But she didn't tell them the reason. He had a heart condition and didn't know how much longer he could keep working. So, when the couple were divorced, they decided she should have the house and 90 per cent of the savings. That way, she and the children wouldn't have to depend on his being healthy for their daily bread. "When they understood the reasons behind the agreement," the father said, "our relationship improved and they didn't think I was stiffing them any more."

Another problem that can crop up with stepfamilies is unequal gift-giving by relatives such as grandparents. You can't force grandparents to spend the same amounts on step-grandchildren as they do on grandchildren, but you can talk to them about dividing the bounty a little more evenly and not arousing hostility in stepsiblings.

As time passes, many issues that loom large at the beginning of a remarried relationship may become less threatening. Spouses learn to adapt their different styles of money management, or at least talk openly about them and seek compromises. Stepparents and stepgrandparents grow to love the kids, even if they're not related by blood, and become more generous in their support. Children overcome their jealousy of half or stepsiblings, and come to relish the emotional bonds and security of a large family.

A blended family, if it works, can become as cohesive and strong as a nuclear family that remains intact. Perhaps even stronger, because both spouses get a second chance—to improve on mistakes the first time around, to resolve their differences and to build a secure financial future together.

STITCHING YOUR SAFETY NET

If your philosophy is "live for today and let tomorrow take care of itself," then skip this chapter. But if you want to shield yourself and your family against the nasty slings and arrows that life can throw at you, then pay attention to what comes next.

You probably know what you need—an emergency fund, an up-to-date will and power of attorney, and life and disability insurance and household insurance. They are all part of the safety net that cushions you from financial harm when something unpleasant happens at a time you least expect it. They can help make life's disasters a little more bearable.

But knowing you should prepare for bad times is not the same as actually doing it. Most people find it easier to drag their feet and put off making unpleasant decisions—and I'm no exception. I thought about getting a will a dozen times before arranging an appointment with a lawyer. I even wrote articles about it. But, as with many things you dread, the anticipation was worse than the reality. It wasn't such a bad experience.

So, don't feel bad if your safety net has a few holes. Getting the right amount of protection for yourself and your dependents is a daunting task and takes a while to accomplish. And even when the job is done, you can't rest on your laurels. Your needs will change every few years as you get older and so should your cushion. Periodic review is essential.

I'm going to come across here like your conscience—or your mother. Please forgive me. I know it's depressing to think about losing your job, getting ill, being hurt in an accident or dying. We all prefer to look on the bright side. All I can say is that when you confront the worst and put some plans in place, you will feel better and more secure. And one day, your family may thank you for it.

Preparing for an Emergency

What is the worst thing that can happen to a family? From a financial point of view, it is the sudden and unexpected loss of an essential income. Ask a financial planner how much money you should have on hand to see you through an emergency and the likely answer is: enough to cover three to six months' worth of living expenses. You will also be told to keep the money in safe investments that pay a fairly low return so you can cash them in at a moment's notice.

But for many people, this advice simply doesn't work. If you have an after-tax income of $40,000 a year, you will need $10,000 to $20,000 in cash to meet expenses for a quarter to half a year. But you're probably spending all or most of your income, so how can you save such a large amount?

Moreover, by keeping the money in liquid investments, you will earn only 3 to 4 per cent on your savings in today's market—and part of that will be taken away by income tax. Meanwhile, you will pay 8 to 10 per cent on your mortgage and 15 to 18 per cent on your credit cards. You are losing money when you keep cash in the bank rather than using it to pay off your debts.

So, a growing number of advisors are abandoning the standard formula and encouraging people to structure their assets so they can get at them in an emergency—without insisting that they set aside so much cash. It's also important to realize that untapped borrowing power is the same as money in the bank when it comes to handling a financial crisis.

First go through the "what if" exercises to see how bad things would be if you or your spouse lost your jobs. How tough would it be to find another job? Could you get along on one salary for a few months? If not, how big a shortfall would there be?

Second, consider what borrowing power you can mobilize if your income is slashed. If you have been paying off your mortgage, as well as investing money for your children's education and for retirement, you probably have some valuable assets that can be sold, refinanced or pledged as collateral for a loan.

Start with the family home. If your house is worth $250,000 in today's market and you have a $150,000 mortgage, you have up to $100,000 in home equity that can be tapped in an emergency.

Some ways to do this:

- You can add a second mortgage, say for $25,000, and use the cash to tide you over.
- You can discharge the existing mortgage and take out a new mortgage of $175,000. You keep the extra $25,000 as above, but the advantage is that a first mortgage carries a lower interest rate than a second.
- You can extend the time to pay off the loan. If your mortgage has 10 years to run, ask the lender to refinance based on a 15-year or 20-year time span. This will lower the payments and give you extra cash flow.

When negotiating with a mortgage lender, watch out for prepayment penalties. They can hit you hard if you have a five-year mortgage term with three or four years left to run. The closer you are to renewal, the less costly it will be to refinance. If your lender imposes a stiff penalty, another lender may be more cooperative. Shop around.

You can also take out a personal line of credit, using your home as collateral. It is important to arrange one before a crisis strikes, since you may not have enough income to qualify afterward. The line of credit will be registered as a second mortgage on your property, but it offers more flexibility than a mortgage.

The interest rate on a secured line of credit is set at or just above the bank's prime lending rate—much lower than the second mortgage rate. You pay a minimum amount every month, which can be interest only, so your out-of-pocket cost will be lower.

And with a line of credit, you pay only for what you use. If you have arranged a $50,000 credit line but you need only $20,000, you pay interest only on $20,000. The other $30,000 is there in reserve for another emergency later on.

But a large line of credit can be dangerous and easily misused. Imagine someone handing you $50,000 in borrowing power. If you're not strict about reserving it for a bona fide crisis, you can quickly spend right up to your limit on vacations, entertaining and home decoration. Then your credit will be exhausted when you really need it. Self-discipline is essential. If you can't handle temptation, forget the line of credit and build an emergency fund through gradual savings.

After your house, the next most valuable asset may be your registered retirement savings plan. Obviously, it's better to leave your RRSP alone until you retire, but that's not always possible in an emergency. You will have tax deducted on the amount you withdraw, but if your income is low you will get most or all of the tax back. The goal is to remove enough from the RRSP to get you through a rough patch and rebuild the fund later on.

If you cash in an RRSP in a year when your income is low, you will pay little or no tax on the money. There is an up-front withholding tax (ranging from 10 to 30 per cent), but you will get the money back when you file your income tax return. Make sure some of the RRSP funds are liquid, not tied up in long-term deposits, so you can get at them in a hurry.

An RRSP cannot usually serve as collateral for a loan. But if it is registered as a trust, you can use it to secure a loan if your administrator agrees. Your income for the year will be increased by the value of the collateral, so you'll pay more tax. Later, when you repay the loan, you will get an offsetting deduction.

Money you have put aside for your children's education can be another source of cash in a crisis. Collapsing a registered education savings plan is not advisable, since you get your own contributions back but none of the interest earned. However, if the money is not registered and is in a bank account, life insurance policy or mutual funds—and if your child is still many years away from college—you may want to cash it in or borrow against it. Or you can suspend the monthly payments until your finances are in better shape.

Try not to fall back on credit cards for emergency borrowing. They are handy, that's for sure, and tempting. The credit limit is usually generous, and if you accidentally exceed it, the bank or trust company may give you a higher limit, no questions asked. But with their high double-digit interest rates, credit cards are an expensive source of credit, much more costly than a personal loan or line of credit. If you have a large credit card balance, try to refinance it at a lower rate.

Sometimes, you can get a bank loan without pledging any assets at all. If your banker thinks you are a good credit risk, you can borrow money on the strength of your character alone or your net worth. This is certainly a route worth exploring.

I'm not saying there is no need for an emergency fund. Everyone should have a cushion for unexpected expenses.

Buy Canada Savings Bonds each fall, since they are cashable on demand, or arrange an automatic transfer from your chequing account into a savings account or money market fund. This money will be a godsend when you need to patch a leaky roof, replace a car's transmission or send kids on a school trip.

But it is an unrealistic and unwise use of your savings to accumulate enough to cover three to six months of expenses in a low-interest account. The best advice is to save for the long term. Focus on paying off the mortgage, building a retirement fund and financing the children's education. Then, tap this equity to get you through a crisis.

Writing a Will

If you don't have a will, you should get one as soon as you start a family. A will tells those left behind how you want to divide your assets, who will care for your young children if you and your spouse are no longer there and at what age you want them to inherit.

Only half of adult Canadians have a will, according to a survey by the Trust Companies Association of Canada. You may think you have no assets, so drafting a will is an unnecessary expense. Or you may dread making tough decisions about a world in which you are no longer around. If you're superstitious, you may worry that preparing a will hastens your death—just like washing your car invariably brings on rain.

But having a will is like stockpiling earthquake supplies: as soon as you get yourself prepared for the Big One, you have less anxiety about its happening. Ideally, your will won't be needed for the next 50 years, but at least it's done.

I am embarrassed to say my husband and I were among the will-less group until our older son was 12. A lawyer we knew kept calling us and scolding us about procrastinating, until we finally ran out of excuses and had to do it. The process was like running a long-distance race—painful while it lasted but an exquisite relief once it was over.

If you die without a will, or intestate, your assets will be divided up according to law, resulting in a division that may be unfair. Each province has different rules about who inherits when there is no will. In general, only blood relatives, those legally married and those legally adopted can inherit. Common-law relationships are not recognized for the purposes of succession, but unmarried partners can apply for a share of the estate in some instances.

Suppose you are single, with no spouse or children. When you die, your estate will pass to your closest surviving relative. Parents are given top priority, and if they are no longer living, the assets go to any brothers or sisters. Nephews and nieces are next on the list, after which any surviving next of kin has a claim. If no one can be found, the government takes everything. Friends cannot inherit.

As the family gets larger, intestacy rules get more complex, and the rules vary widely from one province to another. For example, if you leave your spouse and one child, Newfoundland and P.E.I. laws divide the estate equally between them. In Quebec, the spouse gets one-third of the estate and the children get the rest. In Manitoba, the spouse inherits everything and the children nothing.

If there is more than one child, the balance in most provinces shifts away from the spouse in favour of the children. In Ontario, for example, the spouse gets the first $75,000. This is about to change in the province, with the spouse's preferential share being significantly increased. The balance is divided one third to the spouse, two thirds to the children.

When there is no will, the distribution of your assets is always immediate. The property is simply handed over to the beneficiaries for them to do with as they please. This can cause problems if you die leaving young children. The child's shares of the estate must be paid into court, and the surviving parent or guardian will not have control over the funds. As soon as the child reaches the age of majority, he or she can then apply to get all the money.

An 18-year-old may not be ready to handle large sums of money responsibly. Most parents prefer to dole out an inheritance in stages—perhaps waiting until their children are 25 or older to give them any substantial amounts. To do that, you have to leave instructions in a will for a delayed or staggered distribution.

Choosing a Guardian

Another reason why parents need a will is to choose a guardian for their children. This is someone you would like to bring up your kids in case you and your spouse both die—unlikely, but not unheard of. Your wishes are not binding, but will be taken into account in deciding who gets custody of any kids under 18 at the time of your death.

Suppose you decide your brother and sister-in-law are the best people to look after your child and you appoint them as guardians in your will. This appointment lasts for a certain amount of time after your death (90 days in Ontario), then they have to apply to the courts to be legally appointed. The court decides what is in the child's best interests and may want to hear the child's views on the matter.

Perhaps more important, your will can name anyone you do *not* want appointed as guardian. Although it won't preclude their appointment, "it will put the court on notice to scrutinize closely an application for custody by that individual," says Toronto estate lawyer Barry Corbin.

How do you choose a legal guardian? Draw up a list of desirable parenting traits and then choose a couple you know who most closely matches it. Besides a proven track record as a parent, you want someone who has some skills in handling money and is well known to you and your children. Take into account the age of your children and where they are growing up. How would they handle a move to another city and the loss of their friends after the death of their parents?

It is always possible that the person you choose will not be able to care for your children when the need arises, so don't forget to name one or more alternates. And before appointing any guardians, make sure you discuss it with them first. You're handing over a great responsibility and you want to know they will raise your children the same way you would.

Sometimes, the best way to line up guardians is through a reciprocal arrangement. You approach friends or relatives who are also parents and suggest you will look after their kids if they'll look after yours. Make sure they are aware of the responsibilities involved; this is not an honorary job like being a godparent. But remind them that chances are very slight that they will be called upon to fulfill their duties.

Choosing an Executor

Another person to designate in your will is an executor, someone who will take over your financial affairs and administer your estate after you die. This involves paying your outstanding debts and taxes, identifying and gathering your assets and distributing them according to the wishes laid out in your will.

The executor and the guardian do not have to be the same person. In fact, it may be better to appoint different people in each role to avoid conflicts of interest. The executor can oversee how the guardian spends your money on the care of the children.

Who should be your executor? Ideally, someone trustworthy who knows you and your family, has good business sense and lives nearby. If no individual fits the bill, you might want to name two or more people as co-executors. One of them can be your spouse.

Again, check with the people to see if they're willing to accept the job. In the Trust Companies Association survey, one-third of those with wills did not bother to discuss the contents with the person they named as executor. Your chosen executors need to know what is in your will to be able to gauge how much work is involved.

Only 6 per cent of Canadians name a lawyer, accountant or trust company as their executor, the survey found. The vast majority (77 per cent) choose a member of the immediate family. Trust companies are eager to take on the job of executor, saying they have the training, resources and continuity of personnel to ensure your instructions are carried out. They offer to help prepare your will in the hope of being named as executor and earning the fees that go with the job.

Unless your estate is too large and complex for surviving friends or relatives to administer, you don't need a professional executor. Ignore the trust company appeals and stick with people you know and trust. They can call on professionals for any technical advice they need. Family members are less likely to take a chunk of the estate as compensation. Chances are they will try to leave as much as possible for your intended beneficiaries.

By law, executors are entitled to compensation for the work they do. The courts generally award about 5 per cent of the estate's value. This is extremely generous for the time and trouble of being an executor, says lawyer Ashton Winter of Port Dover, Ontario, who thinks trust companies should be used only as a last resort. Dealing with them is "often expensive, time-consuming, awkward and frustrating." Many lawyers and heirs agree with his views.

Costs

How much does it cost to prepare a will? You can do it yourself without incurring any legal costs. A "holograph" will—one that is entirely in your own handwriting and on a blank sheet of paper with no letterhead—is legally effective in most provinces. It must be signed by you and requires no witnesses. You can also buy a fill-in-the-blanks will form at a stationery store or use a computer program designed for will drafting. Because this type of will is not entirely in your own handwriting, you will have to get witnesses who are not beneficiaries or the spouse of one.

While relying on a do-it-yourself will is cheaper than paying to have a will drawn up, this may not be the best procedure. If your instructions are unclear and there is a chance of any arguments among the beneficiaries, then it is better to go to a lawyer to have one prepared. Lawyers are trained to avoid ambiguities, ensure the bequests are legal and save your estate and heirs from unnecessary taxation. Wills are often a "loss leader" for lawyers who take reduced fees in order to get new clients and spinoff business.

If you and your spouse or partner have a fairly straightforward financial situation, you can expect to pay about $250 to $500 for a pair of wills. It can be more expensive for your family if you don't have a will. Your estate will be in limbo until the court appoints an administrator, who must post a bond as a form of insurance to protect the assets unless a court orders otherwise. This can cost the estate from $500 to $1,000 a year. On the other hand, an executor named in a will is not required to post such a bond (unless he or she lives in a foreign country).

What You'll Need to Know

Before you go to see a lawyer about a will, here are some things you should do:

- Make a list of everything you own of significant value, such as savings accounts, RRSPs, investments, pensions and real estate. The list should include details of where the assets are located. If a financial institution is involved, what are the account numbers? Do you have a safety deposit box and who has the keys? Where is the deed to the house?

- Make a list of items that have sentimental value and decide who should get them after your death. If a friend collects china, you may want to leave him or her your best dishes. Your nephew, who enjoys golf, may be happy to inherit your clubs. Don't leave out your cherished, though perhaps inexpensive, possessions.
- Are any of your assets owned jointly with a spouse or partner? If so, the list should indicate this. Married or common-law couples often register their homes and cottages in their two names as joint tenants. This means ownership passes directly to the spouse at death without going through the estate. Bank accounts may also be in joint names. Sometimes, friends buy a property together and own it as joint tenants.
- List all the insurance policies on your life, noting the expected death benefits and who is to receive them. Make sure there is a designated beneficiary on each policy.
- Does your RRSP name a beneficiary? It may be a spouse, a child or another family member. If so, note this fact so there is no conflict with your will. Married couples should name each other as beneficiaries on their RRSP applications, so the money will roll over to the survivor tax-free and won't become part of the estate.
- Record the amounts you owe and that others owe you. If you would like all your debts to be paid at your death, ensure that your estate will have enough liquid assets to do so. If not, you will need life insurance to make up the difference.
- Where do you want your estate to go if both you and your spouse or heirs die at the same time?

- Ask yourself at what age you want your children to inherit. When will they be old enough to handle bequests responsibly? You may decide, for example, to give your children one-third of their inheritance at age 18, one-third at 25 and the rest at 30.

Once your will is completed, do *not* keep it in a safety-deposit box at a bank or trust company. These boxes are usually sealed at your death. Keep the original in a safe place at home or with your lawyer. Make sure the executor knows where it is.

Review your will every few years, especially when there has been a change in your family circumstances (births, deaths, disabilities, marriages, separation or divorce). A major increase or decrease in your net worth is also a reason to review your estate plans. And periodic calls to your lawyer will determine if changes in tax or family laws will affect your arrangements.

Arranging a Power of Attorney

When seeing a lawyer about a will, it's a good idea to get a power of attorney at the same time. This costs $50 to $150, depending on complexity. Unlike a will that kicks in after you die, a power of attorney is intended to be used while you're alive. It ensures your affairs are handled responsibly if you cannot manage them yourself. (Some provinces do not have power of attorney laws, so check with your lawyer.)

Though it's grisly to contemplate, you may get hit by a bus one day and become totally disabled. If your illness drags on, your spouse may need to empty your bank account, liquidate your investment portfolio or sell the family house. Without a power of attorney, this would not be possible—even if the savings, investments and real estate are held in joint tenancy in both names.

By executing an "enduring" or "durable" power of attorney, so called because it continues in force once you become mentally incompetent, you can appoint someone to act when you can't. Without a power of attorney, your spouse will have to apply to the court for the right to make financial decisions on your behalf, a time-consuming and expensive process. In some cases, a public trustee may be appointed to handle your affairs.

The main concern that most of us have with power of attorney is possible abuse or exploitation. A person acting on your behalf under a power of attorney cannot do everything. He or she is authorized to make financial decisions for you, but cannot change your will or give consent for you for medical care or treatments (see "Preparing a Living Will" below).

To avoid giving too much power to one person, you can name two attorneys who must act jointly, suggests lawyer Barry Corbin. Or you can lodge the power of attorney with a third party, with clear instructions as to when it is to be released. For example, you might specify that the person named to act for you has to provide a written medical opinion that you are no longer able to manage your financial affairs. But keep in mind that such precautions can slow down decision-making at a time when quick action may be crucial.

In 1995, Ontario plans to bring in a tough new law, the Substitute Decisions Act, to cut down on possible abuses of powers of attorney, such as children attempting to take control of an elderly parent's estate. Two witnesses will be required and there are strict criteria on who can be a witness. The cost of getting a power of attorney will rise substantially, lawyers say. So if you live in Ontario, get a power of attorney as soon as possible because documents that were legal before will still stand.

Preparing a Living Will

Unlike your last will and testament, which leaves instructions for survivors after you die, a living will tells your doctor and family members what kind of medical care you want while you are still alive. The "traditional" living will is intended to express your desire not to have your life prolonged by artificial means if you are terminally ill. Both Richard Nixon and Jacqueline Kennedy Onassis had living wills instructing that treatment be cut off when they were close to death.

Living wills are legally binding in some Canadian provinces, such as Nova Scotia, Manitoba and Quebec. Ontario has passed a law, which has not come into force yet. If a living will has no legal status, is there a reason to make one? Yes, since the Canadian Medical Association has endorsed a policy supporting living wills and most doctors abide by them. Your doctor and family members may follow your written directions out of a sense of moral obligation when the time comes to make a decision and you cannot give your own consent to treatment.

A more sophisticated document than a living will is an advance health care directive. (Again, this is not yet recognized in law. Ontario's new Substitute Decisions Act and Consent to Treatment Act will give it legal force.) It is not restricted to terminal conditions and allows you to specify which of several treatments you want applied in a given medical scenario. Do you want an organ transplant, for example, or cardiac resuscitation? You can also name a surrogate to make decisions for you when you can no longer do so.

Your surrogate or proxy in making medical care decisions should be someone you know and trust, such as a spouse, partner, family member or close friend. It is important to ask them in advance if they are willing to take on the job and tell them what your wishes are. You can appoint more than one person to be your proxy, but make it clear if they are to act together or if one takes over from the other. If they are to act together, how are any disagreements to be resolved?

Most people will wait to draw up a living will until they become sick, but you can do it at any time. You don't have to draft your own. Your lawyer can probably provide one and, in some provinces, the government has produced standard forms you can use. You should probably review it with your doctor, who can tailor it to your own health situation.

You can order a living will for $5 from the Centre for Bioethics, University of Toronto, 88 College St., Toronto, Ont. M5G 1L4, telephone (416) 978-2709. A more detailed advance health care directive is available to members of Dying with Dignity, 600 Eglinton Ave. East, Suite 401, Toronto, Ont. M4P 1P3, telephone (416) 486-3998. Membership costs $30 a year.

It's best to let as many people as possible know the contents of your living will. Make copies for your doctor, lawyer, family and your wallet. Don't put it in your safety-deposit box, since it may not be easy to get hold of the document when needed.

Review your living will periodically and update it if you change your mind about your treatment choices or your proxy. Sign and date the new document and send it to the same people who received the original. Changes in your family situation, such as divorce or separation or a move to a new city, may prompt a review. If you are admitted to hospital, discuss your living will with your doctor there.

Buying Life Insurance

Unless you are very wealthy, you probably need some life insurance to safeguard your family's financial future in case of your death. The right amount of insurance will replace your income, pay off your mortgage and send your children to college. The trick is deciding how much insurance is enough and not getting too little or too much.

As soon as children are born, you start hearing from insurance agents who track down prospects from newspaper birth announcements. Most of us buy life insurance from agents and brokers, who are trained to analyse needs and recommend certain types of coverage. But you can also buy insurance from banks and trust companies and even through the mail.

Mail order is the route Edward and I chose. We bought a term insurance plan through the University of Toronto alumni association, picking the coverage we wanted without having to sit down with an agent and hear a sales pitch. Each year, the renewal arrives in the mail and we send off a cheque. No one ever calls and suggests we buy more. (We obviously like a hands-off arrangement, since our car and home insurance coverage is also provided by direct insurers, with no agent in the middle.)

You may prefer to have a closer relationship with someone who can explain the policy intricacies to you. Before you sit down with an insurance agent, take time to figure out your needs. It's not hard to do with a simple worksheet provided by the Canadian Life and Health Insurance Association. The free consumer guide, "Sharpen Your Pencil: How Much Life Insurance is Enough," is available from the CLHIA at 1-800-268-8099, or (416) 777-2344 in Toronto.

Estimating Life Insurance

A rule of thumb for working out how much life insurance you need is to take your family's after-tax annual income and multiply it by five, eight or ten. But everyone's circumstances are different, so it's safer to take a few extra minutes and do a more detailed calculation.

Start by deciding how much money your family might require over the years if you or your spouse or partner were no longer around. You may want to include the following expenses:

- Medical, legal and funeral costs relating to death.
- Probating the will and possible executor's fees, plus bequests in the will.
- Income taxes payable at death, including capital gains tax on the estate, and accounting fees.
- Paying off an uninsured mortgage on the family home and other outstanding loans.

- Funding the children's education.
- Retirement income for the surviving spouse or partner, plus further education or training (if needed) to increase his or her earnings potential.

In figuring total need, don't ignore the contributions of a stay-at-home parent. If he or she is no longer there, the family will have to pay for replacement services such as child care, meal preparation and home maintenance. This could amount to $20,000 or more in the early years. As time passes, the cost should go down as the children grow up and new family patterns emerge.

After you have computed this rough and no doubt daunting projection of your family's needs, you're ready to calculate the plus side of the equation. Add up the resources your family will have during this same period. They include:

- The surviving spouse or partner's income.
- Existing life insurance, including group insurance plans at work.
- Death benefits from an employer pension plan or the Canada Pension Plan/Quebec Pension Plan.
- The maturity value of any registered education savings plans. If you have purchased optional life insurance, the RESP will stay in force and payments will continue to be made after your death.
- Investments such as stocks, bonds or mutual funds.
- The value of your house, if sold to generate income.
- Your registered retirement savings plan, if cashed in. (But remember, the money can be rolled over tax-free into your spouse's RRSP.)

As a final step, subtract your total assets from total liabilities. The shortfall between what you have and what you need should be funded by life insurance. An insurance agent or financial advisor will help you figure out what policy amount, when invested, will meet your needs.

Types of Life Insurance

There are about 150 life insurance companies in Canada, each offering a slew of products with fancy names. But the main thing to remember is that there are only two types of policies: those that pay out money to your dependents when you die (term policies), and those that cover your dependents and offer some sort of savings or investment plan (whole life, permanent, cash value or universal life policies).

If you can't seem to save any other way, you might look into the second type of policy. The attraction is that you build up some equity if you don't die during the coverage period and if your insurance needs outlast your children's adolescence. Universal life insurance is often pitched as a way to save for education and does offer certain tax benefits (see chapter 6).

For most young families, with big mortgages to pay and other financial priorities, a term policy will do just fine. Marlys Harris, a senior writer at *Money* magazine, suggests that insurance policies are like condoms. You don't buy them for the package or the extras; you buy them for pure protection.

Term is by far the cheaper option. You buy it for specific periods, after which you renew. The cost at renewal time gets higher as you get older and become more of a risk. It's designed to pay off only if you die prematurely. There is no cash value or savings in the policy that you can borrow against or withdraw.

Agents prefer to sell cash value policies, since they earn far lower commissions on term policies. They will give you a variety of reasons why term insurance is inferior to a forced savings plan. The two main arguments are that term insurance gets very expensive in your later years, and that you're throwing money down the drain because there's no buildup of cash values.

The answer to the first argument is that life insurance is something you need when you have a young family and big debts. As you get older, you may not require as much insurance or even any at all. Your income will be greater, your children will be self-sufficient and your mortgage will eventually be paid off.

As for wasting money, it's true there's no payoff if you don't die while you're insured. But so what? Car and home insurance work the same way. If there are no accidents or disasters, you pay for coverage and get nothing in return. You join an automobile club, but if your car doesn't break down or need towing, there goes your membership fee. Or you buy an extended warranty on an appliance that never malfunctions. Insurance is expensive, but the trade-off is peace of mind.

Meanwhile, you will pay dearly for cash value policies at the time when you need life insurance most. Take, for example, a 40-year-old man who buys insurance with a $500,000 death benefit. He pays an initial premium of $795 for a 10-year term policy, compared with $2,200 for a cash value policy. The saving in buying term is $1,405, which can make a huge difference in cash flow at that stage of life.

Over the man's lifetime, the term policy will end up costing more. After 30 years, he will have paid $100,200 for the term insurance, compared with $66,000 for the cash value policy. But that assumes he will still need a half-million-dollar insurance policy as he ages. Many people find they can do with less coverage as their net worth increases.

The above example is from an excellent book, *Insure Sensibly: A Guide to Life and Disability Insurance,* by James Bullock and George Brett. It's worth reading if you want an unbiased view of the subject.

Because of the problem of rising rates for term insurance, many companies have introduced a type of policy called term-to-100. Renewal rates stay constant as long as the policy stays in force, but you pay for the privilege in higher premiums. If you think you may need lifetime coverage, this is a better way to go than pure term.

When buying term insurance, make sure it has a guaranteed right of renewal. This means it can be renewed for another term without medical evidence of insurability. The insurance company should also guarantee the future cost of your insurance. The premiums you will pay as you get older should be spelled out in the policy. If the renewal rates are not guaranteed, you could face huge increases in your insurance costs.

A term policy should also be convertible. This means it can be changed to a permanent policy without providing proof of health. Convertibility is important if you later develop a medical problem and become uninsurable, or if you need permanent insurance to cover capital gains tax at your death.

Two-income families should ask about a type of joint policy called first to die. In the past, agents sold insurance to the male breadwinner and didn't bother insuring the housewife's income. But today, many couples have two roughly equal incomes. A first to die policy pays out automatically at the death of one spouse, thus avoiding the need to take out two policies that cost more. Not only married couples but also common-law and same-sex couples can buy these policies. They can also be used to insure business partners.

There can be a problem with first to die policies, however, if the marriage or common-law relationship breaks down. You will have to get a new individual policy, which may be hard to do if you are not in good health. It may be safer to own two policies, which will continue no matter what happens to the relationship. Another type of policy is "joint and second to die" insurance. This is intended to pay the taxes on property or RRSPs belonging to the couple on the death of the surviving spouse.

Choosing a Broker

How do you find a good agent or broker? Ask friends and relatives for referrals. It can be risky to deal with someone who comes knocking at your door to solicit business. The life insurance industry is notorious for taking in all comers and spitting them out a short while later. New agents give up after selling policies to all their friends and relatives, and few last beyond five years.

In such a revolving-door business, look for a track record of five to ten years of service and get names of satisfied clients you can call. Check to see if the agent or broker has a professional designation, such as Chartered Life Underwriter (C.L.U.) or Chartered Financial Consultant (Ch.F.C.). Fewer than half the agents selling life insurance have both these courses.

If you are buying term insurance, find a broker who subscribes to a computerized pricing service and can quote rates for various insurance companies. For example, Compulife Software in Kitchener, Ontario keeps tabs on about 50 insurers dealing through brokers. A new company, Insurance Quote Services of Canada, in Richmond Hill, Ontario, provides term insurance rates to the public on a toll-free line (1-800-363-8089). The company earns commissions if it sells policies, just like any other insurance agent.

When a broker quotes rates, ask about a company's financial stability. There have been several well-publicized failures of Canadian life insurers in recent years and a few big bailouts. With 150 life insurance companies operating in Canada, there is expected to be a shakeout in the next few years. Some will merge and some will die. To check on a company's health, read its annual reports for a few years and check with rating agencies such as Dominion Bond Rating Service, Canadian Bond Rating Service and TRAC Insurance Services.

The LIFE TRAC Report is a financial analysis of all federally licensed life insurance companies in Canada and sells for

$600. But for $50, you can get the information on a company of your choice. It has a company profile, early warning solvency test explanations and recommended consumer action. For information, write to TRAC at 133 Richmond St. West, Suite 600, Toronto, Ont. M5H 2L3, telephone (416) 363-8266.

To be on the safe side, stay within the limits guaranteed by the industry's compensation fund. Set up in 1990, the Canadian Life and Health Compensation Corp. (or CompCorp) reimburses consumers if a company collapses. It covers up to $200,000 in death benefits for a life insurance policy, $60,000 for a registered retirement savings plan and $2,000 per month for a life annuity or disability income policy. If necessary, divide your business among two or more companies to avoid exceeding the limits. But remember that this is more expensive than buying insurance from one company.

Don't put too much faith in the compensation fund. It's new, small and lacks legal clout. If there is a large failure, it is doubtful whether the industry could collect enough from members to cover all the losses. The Canada Deposit Insurance Corp., which protects deposits at banks and trust companies, is backed by the resources of the federal government. The insurance fund is not.

Bank Insurance vs. Life Insurance

Suppose you have a mortgage and a young family. Should you buy mortgage insurance through a bank or trust company, rather than buying an individual life insurance policy? If you can afford only one type of insurance, it's probably best to cover your mortgage first since it may be your biggest financial responsibility.

Bank insurance is often cheaper than individual insurance. However, rates are not guaranteed, and the policy may be cancelled at any time. (Individual policies cannot be cancelled by the life insurance company as long as you pay the premium.) Bank coverage is not convertible to any other type of insurance and is not available after age 65.

With a bank plan, the insurance coverage decreases as your outstanding loan decreases and payments stay the same over the life of the mortgage. With a term insurance policy, coverage stays the same and rates rise every few years.

If a husband and wife are both insured and both die at the same time, a bank plan will cover only the outstanding mortgage amount. But if the couple owns a joint policy issued through an insurance company, the death benefit will be paid twice. This will provide enough money to discharge the mortgage and provide for the children as well.

It's rare for couples to die in a common accident, but it can happen. So, if you name your spouse as beneficiary of an insurance policy, you should name an alternate beneficiary as well. If you don't, the insurance proceeds will be included in your estate, exposing your survivors to administrative delays, liability issues and probate fees.

Group Life

Suppose you have group life insurance through your employer and think this will be enough to cover your family's needs. The amount rarely adds up to five or ten times your salary, the amount you probably need. But even if it does, you have no control over it. If you are laid off or quit, you will no longer be covered by life insurance. You may have the right to convert it to expensive permanent insurance, but term-to-100 is usually not an option. And the insurance can be suspended during a strike or cancelled altogether if the company is going through hard times.

For most people with salaried jobs and young dependents, it's better to have an individual life insurance policy and top it up with the group plan. Then, if you lose your job, your private coverage will be in place and you can bump up the coverage.

Buying Disability Insurance

Most people insure their lives, houses and cars but don't think about protecting their most valuable asset—their ability to earn a living. Over the years this can add up to millions of dollars. And statistics show there is far greater risk of becoming disabled during your working years than of dying prematurely.

Disability insurance is designed to replace your income if you have an illness or injury that prevents you from working. It complements your life insurance, since the benefits kick in while you're still alive but unable to support your family.

Disability coverage is even more important if you are self-employed, because your partners, employees and creditors depend on your ability to work. When you are too ill to do your job, routine business bills can quickly eat up your investments, RRSPs and even your home equity. "And if you miss quarterly income tax installments, Revenue Canada can demand full payment *plus interest* after one year...and garnishee disability benefits," warns the Canadian Life and Health Insurance Association.

Experience shows that nearly a third of all people now aged 35 will be unable to work for at least six months before reaching age 65. If a disability lasts three months, chances are it will last three years or more for a 35-year-old man or woman and four years or more for a 45-year-old man or woman. Can your assets last that long?

You probably have disability coverage through your employer, union or professional association, as well as benefits through government programs such as workers' compensation, unemployment insurance and the Canada/Quebec Pension Plan. Some plans supplement each other and will not pay unless coverage runs out elsewhere. Some disability benefits are taxable and some are not. It's all very confusing.

The self-employed can join associations that offer group disability coverage, such as a Chamber of Commerce or Board of Trade. But if they cannot get group insurance, they have to buy an individual policy. Well-heeled executives and professionals may also need their own coverage, since the benefits from a group plan are often too low to live on. "Those with incomes exceeding $400,000 or $500,000," says insurance broker James Bullock, "could receive as little as 25 per cent of their working income. The proportion of coverage decreases as income increases."

As with life insurance, you have to look at the big picture. The way to start is to haul out your company brochures to see what you and your spouse are covered for. Then, take the time to fill in some worksheets that help you calculate your income needs and compare your expenses with your existing resources. A good source of help is the Canadian Life and Health Insurance Association's booklet "Disability Insurance: Where Will the Money Come From If You're Disabled?" It's free for the asking from the Information Centre, CLHIA, 1 Queen St. East, Suite 1700, Toronto, Ont. M5C 2X9, telephone 1-800-268-8099.

Even if you have reasonable disability coverage at work, it is sensible to add an individual policy to your group plan. The reason is that if you are laid off, it's difficult to keep the same coverage. Few group disability policies can be converted to individual plans. (However, there are some policies designed to bridge the gap between the time you leave work and take up another job.) And your new employer may not provide a group insurance plan.

Many group plans provide minimal coverage. For example, they can cut off benefits if you are too ill to perform your own job but able to do other work. You may be forced to take a job that does not match your skills and pays less than what you were making before. If you buy an individual policy, you can choose the right to return only to your former occupation or receive benefits that last for life.

Disability insurance rarely covers more than 70 per cent of your former income. Insurers want to give you an incentive to get back to work quickly. So you may be forced to scrimp and save while living on less than you did before.

If your employer has paid part or all of the premiums, the disability benefits will be taxed in your hands. However, if you paid the premiums yourself, there will be no tax on the benefits—and that's a real advantage, since it puts more cash in your pocket.

Besides group insurance through work and government programs, or if you're self-employed, you may have other sources of income that can help ease the cash crunch if you are disabled:

- Many professional and business associations and university alumni groups offer disability insurance to their members. But the premiums increase as you get older and you may have to provide medical evidence of insurability at renewal.
- Automobile insurance policies pay income replacement benefits if you are injured in a car accident, but the amount may be low. The auto insurance is supposed to be secondary to any other disability income plan.
- Banks, trust companies and credit unions offer disability protection for consumer loans and mortgages. If you cannot work because of illness, your loan payments are covered. Some plans pay your loan out in full, but you have to be totally and permanent disabled to qualify.
- Many life insurance policies offer a waiver of premium feature. This lets you stop making premium payments but maintain coverage if you are disabled for at least six months. And many companies now offer "living benefits," essentially partial prepayments of death benefits to policyholders who are terminally ill.
- Department stores and oil companies solicit their credit card holders to buy group accident and sickness insur-

ance for pennies a day. These policies should be examined carefully. They may pay a set amount (say $50 a day) if you are hospitalized, yet some disabled people are never admitted to hospital. And some plans cover only accidents, whereas the vast majority of disabilities are caused by illness.

If your existing sources of insurance are not enough, you can top them up with an individual long-term disability policy. But remember the income limits: you can never get more from adding one insurance policy to another than what you were earning at work. People with incomes above $100,000 will be hit by ceilings that restrict coverage to just 25 or 50 per cent of their working income.

Most life insurance agents and brokers sell disability insurance, but only a handful of companies underwrite these plans. The market is split among Paul Revere Life Insurance, Great-West Life Assurance and Provident Life & Accident Insurance. The industry's association (CLHIA) can give you a complete list.

When shopping around, here are some questions to ask:

- What percentage of my income does this cover? Is there a dollar limit? How is it coordinated with other plans?
- When do benefits begin? How long is the waiting period?
- How long do benefits run? Are they taxable? Are they indexed for inflation?
- What is the definition of disability? Will I get benefits until I am able to do my own job? Till what age? (Age 65 is usually the maximum.) Or will coverage stop once I can return to any suitable occupation ?
- Am I covered for stress-related ailments, drug and alcohol abuse or mental disorders? Many insurers have tightened up coverage because of escalating costs, but you

shouldn't buy a policy that has these exclusions. Prepare to be questioned on your hobbies, work habits and lifestyle, warn James Bullock and George Brett. Insurance companies are cautious about insuring applicants who admit to working long hours and never taking vacations.

- Is the policy guaranteed renewable and non-cancellable? You want to be sure your coverage will be renewed as long as you pay the premiums, without having to submit proof of health, and costs won't go up.
- Can you return to work part-time without losing all your benefits? Some policies make up the difference between what you are earning if you go back to work gradually, while building up your strength, and what you would be getting from the disability insurance plan.
- Is rehabilitation offered? What benefits are paid during rehabilitation? How much is paid if you return to work on a trial basis?
- If your income increases and you want additional coverage, do you have to undergo another physical? This is important because you may have acquired some health conditions since you bought the policy.

If you are a two-career couple, it's possible that you may both be disabled at the same time. To cover yourself in case of a common accident, add up the long-term disability coverage you get from your employers and subtract it from your monthly expenses. If there is a gap, you may want to insure it.

If you are self-employed, you can tailor an individual plan to meet your requirements. This may include covering business overhead costs, paying deferred income tax and paying down most bank loans, or at least the interest. You may also want a policy that will fund your retirement savings plan while you are disabled, so you will be able to retire after you recover.

Remember that disability insurance is quite expensive. The coverage typically costs more than life insurance, because you are more likely to collect benefits and at a younger age. The better the protection, the higher-priced it will be. The premiums you pay also depend on your age and occupation and the risk involved in your job.

Your gender can also be a factor. Disability premiums are somewhat lower for men than for women, because women tend to take more disability leaves and return to work less quickly. Women shopping for disability insurance might be able to get a better deal if they can find a company charging unisex rates.

How can you keep costs down? You can take a shorter benefit period, specifying that you will get compensated for only three years or five years, rather than to age 65. Or you can wait longer for benefits to start. A waiting period of 30 days costs more than stretching it to 90 days. The insurance company figures that the longer you wait, the better the chances your disability will clear up and it won't have to pay at all.

The cost of disability insurance drops dramatically with a longer waiting period, say Mr. Bullock and Mr. Brett. Take the case of a 35-year-old non-smoking man who buys a policy that will pay $2,000 a month to age 65. With a 30-day waiting period, he pays an annual premium of $1,259. His premium drops to $830 if he opts for a 60-day wait, $699 for a 90-day wait and $666 for a 120-day wait. If the insurance premiums are too costly for your budget, they advise, increase your waiting period rather than accept less than all the disability protection available.

Buying Household Insurance

Your most valuable material possessions are probably your home and its contents. Home insurance will protect your belongings from fire, theft and water damage, and help you meet any potential legal obligations arising from injury to others.

Home insurance is important for tenants too. If you rent an apartment, you need to insure the contents since your landlord has no legal responsibility to replace or pay for your personal possessions if they are damaged or destroyed in a natural disaster. And if you have a mishap, for example, a stove that catches fire or a bathtub that leaks to the apartment below you, without liability coverage, you would be responsible for damage to the whole building, not just the space you rent. Your insurance coverage should include the value of any improvements you make, at your expense, to the premises—such as broadloom, built-in cabinets or sound systems.

There are many providers of household and tenant insurance. As with life and disability insurance, you can buy directly from the insurer or go through an independent agent or broker. A discount may be available if you buy both your household and auto insurance through the same broker.

How much insurance you need depends on the value of your belongings. Start by doing an inventory of your household contents, using a notebook, camera, camcorder, tape recorder or preprinted checklist (supplied free by insurance brokers) to document what you own and its value. Be as detailed and descriptive as you can, because after a burglary or fire, you may find it hard to remember everything that disappeared. Complete household records will help you get the best deal from your insurer and will come in handy when you shop to replace the items you lost.

There can be great differences in the type of coverage provided, so you have to ask the right questions and read the policy to see what it includes and excludes. Many property insurance companies base their policies on the clear-language wording developed by the Insurance Bureau of Canada. If you don't understand something or need clarification, ask a broker for help.

How to Get the Best Deal on Home Insurance

Do you want a policy that covers the replacement cost or depreciated value of your belongings? Some policies are more comprehensive than others. Without replacement-cost insurance, you will likely get garage sale prices if an old TV set is stolen or a wornout sofa is ruined. If you want to buy something new instead of something used, it's worth paying a higher premium for replacement-cost coverage. (Many policies today automatically provide it.) But you must actually buy a replacement article to get replacement value from your insurer. If you want a cash settlement, it is usually based on depreciated value.

Another decision: what size deductible do you want? Your insurance policy will require you to pay an agreed amount of certain losses out of your own pocket; the higher the deductible, the lower the premium. On homeowner policies, the deductible will range from $200 to $1,000. Consider upping the deductible if you find the premium cost too high, since you probably won't file a claim unless you have a large loss.

Certain items have limited coverage, regardless of how much your contents are insured for. If you own valuable jewellery, furs, art, antiques, stamp or coin collections, silverware or manuscripts, you should insure them separately through a "floater" policy. (You may need an appraisal to know what they're worth.) A floater usually has no deductible and covers all risks, including mysterious disappearance. If you leave your wedding ring in a shirt pocket, for example, and it vanishes into your washing machine's spin-dry cycle, the insurance will cover your loss. Without a floater, you could collect only if there were a burglary or robbery. Some policies also cover theft with no signs of forced entry.

Often you can negotiate a discount if you install some types of safety equipment, such as a burglar alarm system, deadbolt locks, smoke detectors, fire extinguishers, a timer for lights or motion detector outdoor lights. Ask your insurance broker for details.

If you are self-employed and working at home, check your home insurance policy. There are tight limits on coverage of business equipment (usually up to $1,000 in total), computer software, cash and negotiable securities. You may need a separate business insurance policy, or at least separate coverage for more valuable items. Those under the age of 21, such as children or stepchildren living in your household, are covered under a basic policy for temporary or part-time business pursuits carried out under your roof.

Who is Covered under a Home Insurance Policy?

A policy covers the person or persons named on the coverage summary page. The policy also includes, while living in the same household, the person's spouse, the relatives of either and any person under 21 in their care. Common-law husband-and-wife unions are recognized for insurance purposes if a man and woman have lived together continuously for three years, or for one year if they have a child together. Two people of the same sex living together can get coverage in both their names.

This information comes from the Insurance Bureau of Canada, which has offices in Vancouver, Edmonton, Toronto, Montreal and Halifax. The bureau publishes two helpful brochures for consumers, "Home Insurance and You!" and "Tenant Insuranc, Condominium Insurance and You!", which you can get from insurance brokers or from the bureau's head office at 181 University Ave., 13th floor, Toronto, Ont. M5H 3M7, telephone (416) 362-9528.

Buying Pet Insurance

When thinking about your family's insurance needs, don't forget any four-legged members. If a beloved dog or cat gets hurt in a fight or accident, or contracts a disabling, chronic disease, wait till you see how the veterinarian's bills can add up. Every animal owner can tell you stories. We had a cat who got food poisoning from nibbling at insect traps and had to stay at the vet's for a week till the diarrhea went away. The bill was close to $1,000—and that was a decade ago. Another cat needed extensive dental work because of gum disease. Cost: $250.

Even if you are impervious to a vet's pleas for costly treatment and prepared to write off the family pet, your children won't be. Don't expect them to let Fido or Fuzzy suffer because of a few dollars, or a few hundred dollars. And don't be surprised if youngsters wonder whether you will ditch *them* when they get ill.

In Canada, there is only one insurance policy that covers pets. Pet Plan, which started in 1989, caters strictly to dogs and cats. The animals must be between 12 weeks and eight years old when insurance starts and can remain on it for life. The plan won't cover previously existing illnesses, annual vaccinations, or elective or preventive maintenance such as neutering and routine dental treatment.

For cat owners, a no-frills plan pays up to $650 for each illness and accident, including vet fees, hospitalization and medication. The corresponding plan for dog owners pays up to $750 for each illness. There is a 10 per cent discount for three animals or more. The more elaborate, and more expensive, silver and gold plans also cover boarding fees for the pet if you are unexpectedly hospitalized, holiday cancellation fees if a pet needs life-saving emergency surgery while you're on vacation, the cost of advertising for a lost or stolen pet, and the replacement price of your pet if it is killed in an accident or dies from illness before the age of eight. For information, call Pet Plan at 1-800-268-1169, or write to 50 Burnhamthorpe Rd. West, Suite 700, Mississauga, Ont. L5B 9Z9.

Ask a veterinarian if pet insurance is worthwhile in your case. The exclusion of pre-existing medical conditions can be a real disadvantage, as is the lack of coverage for routine care. But in an emergency, you will be grateful for the insurance.

Our neighbours rave about the plan, since they saved thousands of dollars treating a young dog with a chronic, debilitating illness. With the high cost of veterinary care, they could not have afforded to keep the pet alive and would have had to put it down.

4 AS YOUR PARENTS GET OLDER

Edward and I got married when we were both 26, but like many baby boomers, we came late to parenthood. When our second child was born, we were almost 40. Around the same time, Edward's parents started having serious medical problems. His mother broke her hip, then her ankle, and had to use a wheelchair; his father had a series of strokes and could no longer walk or speak.

Now both 85, my in-laws live in separate old age homes in Toronto. They have been uprooted several times as their health has deteriorated and will undoubtedly have to move again. Troubled by their suffering, Edward and I search constantly for the right institutional environment for them and feel torn by the demands of our parents and our children.

People like us are known as the "sandwich generation," squeezed between parents living into their eighties and nineties and children arriving as we reach middle age. At a time when we should be at the peak of our careers, enjoying some financial success, we feel more pressure on our time and resources. As the meat in the sandwich, we are sliced thinner than ever.

Edward's parents saved enough to finance their own care for the first few years, but their savings—and their children's inheritance— will run out soon. Then we will be caught in a "triple squeeze of financial goals," as U.S. lawyer Adriane G. Berg says in her book *Making Up for Lost Time: Speed Investing for a Secure Future.* Instead of slowing down, we will be forced to work harder and save more to support our parents, build our retirement fund and send our children through university.

If your parents are still alive, no matter whether they are healthy or ailing, it is important to discuss with them the state of their finances and their hopes and plans for the future. You may have responsibilities to carry out, or there may be repercussions that directly affect your family. So, try to find out information about your parents' wills, insurance, pensions and—though the topic is unpleasant in the extreme—their funeral plans.

Few of us feel comfortable talking about money, but it can be even more awkward when the older generation is involved. Playing parent to your parents is no fun, and something Mom or Dad may resist as well. If they brought you up to believe that money talk is vulgar, don't expect them to open up as they get older. You may have to force the issue, to make them confront the need to lift the lid on their finances when they are well, so they can hand over control later when they can no longer cope.

When the topic is aging and death, you may find it extremely difficult to scale the parental wall of silence. Parents may shrug off questions by talking about their wonderful health, while children may feel morbid raising the subject at all, particularly if a large inheritance is involved. When there are several children in a family, parents do not always like to show their hand, fearing sibling rivalry.

As the eldest of four children, I doubt I would get anywhere quizzing my father about his will and estate plans. As he has done all his life, he prefers to keep his financial arrangements to himself, though he confides a little in my brother, who is a chartered accountant. My mother, more open about discussing the future, often asks how to divvy up her jewellery and family heirlooms—questions I find extraordinarily difficult to answer.

Start a frank discussion with your parents about the long-range future. How and where will they live in retirement? What happens if they get sick and can no longer manage independently? Do they have a written will and power of attorney? How do they plan to divide their assets?

To open the lines of communication, approach your parents at a convenient time, perhaps when the family has gathered together for a holiday celebration. Ease into it while you are involved in a relaxed, shared activity, such as playing golf or tennis, slicing vegetables or shovelling snow. If your parents are uncomfortable talking with you about personal finances and find the sudden reversal in roles unsettling, you can send them appropriate books or articles or direct them to investment seminars. Or they can begin by confiding in a lawyer, social worker or financial advisor who specializes in working with retirees or the elderly.

A good way to broach the subject is through your children. Ask your parents if they intend to leave money or set up trusts to provide for their grandchildren after they are gone. Another tack: ask how they handled things when their own parents died, or discuss plans you and your spouse have made for your own deaths.

Or you might get your parents' attention focused on estate planning by talking about taxes. Canada (unlike the United States) does not have death or estate tax. But we do have capital gains tax, which kicks in at death, on the growth of investments such as stocks, bonds, mutual funds and real estate (aside from a principal residence). The tax bite is 35 to 40 per cent at the highest bracket. There is also income tax at death.

So, if a parent leaves a sizable amount to a child—say $200,000 in a registered retirement savings plan or registered retirement income fund (RRIF)—the money is fully taxed as income in the 50-per-cent plus bracket and the child will get less than $100,000 after taxes are paid.

Most provinces also charge probate fees on the value of an estate. Ontario's new fee scale is so hefty—0.5 per cent on estates up to $50,000 and 1.5 per cent of the excess—that it has been criticized as an estate tax in disguise. An Ontario estate valued at $200,000 will attract probate fees of $2,500.

If your parents are worried about taxes eroding the value of what they leave behind, seize the opportunity to discuss ways of cutting the tax bill. There are many planning options, which a competent financial advisor can highlight. In the course of these discussions, parents can reveal the extent of their estate without feeling they are threatened or losing control. "Most parents want their children to get the most money possible," says Ms. Berg. "If there is a way to plan properly, they are usually very receptive to hearing about it."

Estate Planning

Wills

Everyone needs a will, no matter what their age and stage of the game, yet only half of adult Canadians have one. They die leaving a financial mess in their wake. Find out if your parents have prepared their wills and when they did it. (Wills should be reviewed every few years to make sure they are still current.) Ask where they keep their wills. If it is a safety-deposit box, suggest an another location. A person's safety-deposit box is sealed at death, making it difficult for survivors to extricate key documents when they are needed.

A will is particularly important if your parents have remarried. Unless they have named their children as beneficiaries in a new will, the second spouse and his or her children will inherit the bulk of the assets. If there is no will, a prenuptial contract can ensure that assets pass to children from the first marriage. If they didn't sign anything before marriage, they can consider getting a post-nuptial contract.

A parent's will should spell out how jewellery, artwork and items of sentimental value are to be divided up. If you are especially fond of certain possessions, don't feel embarrassed to make your preferences known. Sometimes, speaking up can make a parent's job easier. Peter Volpé, a Toronto financial planner, suggests walking around the family home with your parents to get a feel for how they might want objects dispersed after they die.

In their wills, parents must also name an executor, someone to oversee the estate while it is being settled. Find out who the executor is and if a backup has been appointed. (It's smart to ask potential executors if they want the job, but not everyone bothers to do it.) Parents whose estates are very complex or who worry about family harmony may hire a trust company to fulfill that role. There is a charge for this service, though.

To make the job easier for the executors (since you may be one of them), ask your parents where they keep their assets and financial records. This includes stock and bond certificates, bank accounts, pension plans, insurance policies, retirement funds, property titles, past tax returns and deeds to a cemetery plot. Find out the names of their advisors and the numbers to call in an emergency.

Have they looked at ways to minimize taxes owing at death? When someone dies, they are considered to have sold to their estate their capital property—such as stocks, bonds, mutual funds and real estate—at the current value. The estate must pay tax on the gain in value since the assets were purchased.

If your parents haven't planned properly for the inevitable taxes, their executors may have to sell or mortgage property in the estate to pay Revenue Canada. This whittles away the inheritance that the beneficiaries were meant to enjoy. A professional advisor can calculate the taxes owing at death and show ways to lighten the burden of the final tax bill.

If one parent dies, and leaves assets to the other, there is no capital gains tax owing. But when the survivor dies and leaves assets to the children, tax will be payable at that time. If there is a large estate, parents can help out children with taxes by buying joint life insurance, covering the second-to-die spouse. The insurance proceeds will cover the capital gains tax payable at the death of the surviving spouse.

To lighten the children's tax load, parents can also do an "estate freeze." With this commonly used technique, the worth of an estate is frozen at its current value. If parents live another 20 years, the tax payable at their death will be based on that earlier value. Any further increase in value, and the resulting tax, will become the responsibility of the heirs when they sell the property. Any assets can be frozen—stocks, a cottage, even a family business.

There are other alternatives to leaving property in a will. If your parents have significant assets, they can set up a trust or an investment holding company. Like estate freezes, these plans are complicated and require professional advice. Or parents can name a beneficiary in a life insurance policy, pension plan, RRSP or RRIF. Once they die, the money will be turned over immediately to the beneficiary, thus bypassing the delays and fees involved with probate.

Here's another tactic: a parent can hold a bank account jointly with an adult child. Both have access to the money, and when one dies, the other does not have to wait for the estate to be settled before funds are released. (Quebec is the only province where this arrangement does not apply.)

Power of Attorney

A problem can occur when a parent has a joint bank account with a son or daughter who will get the money automatically when the parent dies. But the parent's will may stipulate that the estate be divided equally among all the children. Since money in the joint account is not part of the estate, the other children will be squeezed out. They will have to split whatever remains in the estate.

For this reason, financial planners suggest that parents give children a power of attorney instead of setting up a joint account. It accomplishes the same purpose, since the child has access to the bank account while the parent is alive. But the money forms part of the estate on death.

Assigning a power of attorney allows older people to make advance provisions for someone to take over their affairs if they can't handle them. They should not wait for a crisis, when they are sick or no longer able to leave the house. Without a power of attorney, the family of an incapacitated adult has to apply to the courts to act on the person's behalf, a long and cumbersome procedure.

But some parents resist the idea—and who can blame them? Letting someone else make financial decisions for you is a serious step that requires careful thinking. In a world where thousands of dollars can be moved from a bank or brokerage account with just one phone call, you really have to trust the person to whom you give this power.

To prevent abuses, it's important to have checks on a power of attorney. Parents can name several children, or they can insist that a child's decisions be reviewed by a trusted lawyer, accountant or financial advisor. They can also limit a power of attorney to a specific time period or a specific function—such as paying bills or depositing cheques when they are out of the country.

You can suggest to your parents that it's a good idea to prepare a power of attorney at the same time they do their will. The document can be kept at the lawyer's office and not released until needed. As an extra safeguard, they can specify that the power of attorney is not valid unless there is a written opinion from a family doctor or a medical specialist that they can no longer handle their affairs.

Parents can also assign a health care power of attorney, giving another person the mandate to make decisions about their medical treatment. Or they can sign a living will, setting out their wishes for intervention if they are terminally ill. Preparing such a document, or even having an informal discussion with you about this topic, will help clear the air and make their wishes known later if they cannot give consent to a life-saving medical procedure. (See chapter 3 for more on powers of attorney and living wills.)

Housing Options for Senior Citizens

Most Canadians stay put after retirement. They continue living in the same home, close to family and friends, and some have a second home down south or in the country. If your parents can handle the costs of home ownership, are healthy and enjoy living on their own, you have no cause to worry. But as they get older, things change. Sooner or later, something has to give—their budget, their health or their ability to live independently. Then you begin your search for housing options.

Here's an idea some of our friends are considering. They are planning to move to a larger house, one with a self-contained apartment for their parents. The idea of "granny flats" is catching on in Canada and many municipalities are changing their bylaws to make them legal. If it works for you, terrific. Your kids are closer to their grandparents, who can also help with babysitting. But it's not the solution for everybody. Some people prefer to keep their distance from their parents and don't relish the thought of sharing the same four walls.

If your parents have a large home and can no longer afford the upkeep, they can rent out rooms to tenants. (But they need the right temperament to be a landlord.) An agency or ad can match them up with people needing accommodation, such as students, retirees or single parents. Home sharing provides elderly owners with companionship, extra security and help with housekeeping, repairs or gardening. Make sure local zoning rules allow it.

Retirees who live in an area where tourists like to visit can open a bed and breakfast establishment. Again, this isn't an answer for everyone. But renting rooms out daily can provide extra income for hospitable types who enjoy meeting people. Your parents might want to sell their current home and buy one more suited to a bed and breakfast clientele.

Reverse Mortgage

A reverse mortgage is an option for people who want to stay in a home they can't afford to maintain. This is a fairly new concept in Canada and has some risks for senior citizens. Financial planners recommend extreme caution. As Montreal financial planner Robert Kerr says in *The Only Retirement Guide You'll Ever Need,* "Do I think the reverse mortgage is a good idea? In general, no, because you should never borrow for personal living costs. There are times when it will be useful, however, such as for short-term arrangements of one to three years, after which moving to a nursing home is expected."

Here's how it works. In general, people must be over 60 years old and own their home outright. The lender advances up to 35 per cent of the appraised value as a mortgage against the home and uses the money to buy an annuity, which will pay an income for life. The borrower can take part of the proceeds as a lump sum.

The advantage? Borrowers make no mortgage payments and get a monthly income that is tax-free. Revenue Canada considers the interest owed on the mortgage as a tax deduction, offsetting the interest earned on the annuity.

But a reverse mortgage is like Pac Man: it can gobble up the house. With no repayments, the interest compounds and the debt rises like a rocket. (That's why the loan covers only a third of the appraised value, leaving a large cushion to protect lenders.) If the homeowner outlives the averages, there is no equity left. When the house is sold or the owner dies, the mortgage is paid off in full and the balance, if any, goes to the owner or the estate.

If the reverse mortgage grows bigger than the house—and this is possible when real estate prices are flat—the borrower does not have to fear being thrown out on the street. The insurance company underwriting the annuity simply swallows the loss, hoping to make it up elsewhere.

But most annuity-based reverse mortgages are profitable for the insurers. For example, a Toronto woman took out a $63,000 reverse mortgage with Security Life in December 1990. She received $10,000 in cash, paid $2,370 in fees, and the remaining $53,000 was used to buy an annuity of $622 a month for life. She died just three years later, after receiving $33,000 in payments. But when the house was sold, the amount owing to the mortgage lender was almost $97,000.

If you are counting on a family home or cottage to be part of a parent's estate, be aware that a reverse mortgage can chew up all the equity and leave nothing behind for the heirs. Explore alternatives, such as a conventional mortgage or home equity line of credit. Though banks dislike lending to retirees, they may feel more secure if an employed son or daughter co-signs the loan.

Reverse mortgage borrowers who want to protect the annuity income should insist on a guarantee period, say 10 or 15 years. If they die prematurely, a lump sum representing the money they would have received over this period will go to their estate. However, the trade-off is that they will have to settle for less money overall. The longer the guarantee period, the lower the monthly payments.

A better solution is a line of credit reverse mortgage, offered by some credit unions. Borrowers control when and how much to withdraw and can make repayments at any time without penalty. This is unlike an annuity-based reverse mortgage, where there can be onerous penalties if the borrower changes his or her mind and tries to cancel the contract before the term is up.

So far, only a few smaller institutions offer reverse mortgages, restricting sales to urban areas in Ontario, Alberta, Quebec and British Columbia. The big banks are sitting on the sidelines, waiting for the government to come in and share the risk. Eventually, observers predict, reverse mortgages will be insured by the Canada Mortgage and Housing Corp., a federal agency. Bankers also say demand is low, since few older people want to assume new mortgages after spending years paying them off.

For an overview of this developing market, a good Canadian source is *Have Your Home and Money Too*, by P.J. Wade. Ms. Wade, a consumer advocate in Toronto, gives potential clients a list of tough questions to ask salespeople and legal advisors. Her philosophy: "A reverse mortgage could be your best friend or your worst enemy. The decision to convert home equity should not be entered into quickly or taken too lightly."

Reverse mortgages have other uses besides allowing senior citizens to stay in their own homes. Parents can use the money for any purpose they like, including helping children or grandchildren achieve their financial goals.

For example, suppose your parents want to stay in their own house and help you buy a house too. They can put a reverse mortgage on their house, using the lump sum to cover your downpayment and the tax-free income to help pay for your mortgage. If they were planning to leave you their house when they died anyway, a reverse mortgage may make some sense. Now, they can see you enjoying the benefits while they are still alive.

In her book, Ms. Wade explores other options besides reverse mortgages for senior citizens who are "house rich and cash poor." For example, some provincial and municipal governments sponsor property tax deferral programs. They allow an older homeowner to put off paying property taxes. Meanwhile, a lien (or legal claim) for the outstanding amount, plus interest, is registered against the home. The lien becomes payable when the home is sold or the owner dies.

Also, a private investor can enter into a sale leaseback plan with an older homeowner. The investor buys the property, then leases it back to the seller for a fixed term of 10 or 20 years, or for life. The investor benefits from any future gain in the value of the property and the seller gets cash, without having to pack one box or sort through one closet. This arrangement is common in farming communities.

Selling the Home

Not all retirees want to hold on to their homes. Many older people solve the housing dilemma by taking a step down. They liberate their home equity and subsidize their retirement by selling and moving to a smaller house or apartment. Some will rent and some will buy. The option they choose depends on how much they hate paying rent cheques each month and never getting anything in return.

My parents did both. After selling their large family home in Montreal, they rented an apartment for 10 years. Then they decided to invest in a condominium apartment, which they have occupied for 10 years. Today, my 77-year-old father is having second thoughts about having so much of his net worth tied up in real estate. Because of overbuilding, condos can be hard to sell.

If your parents are considering buying a condo apartment or townhouse, especially one that is still under construction, they should work with a developer who has a long and untarnished reputation. Examine the company's other developments, Robert Kerr advises, and talk to other owners to see if they are happy with their investment. It's always risky to buy something you can't see. Remember too that owners must pay maintenance fees, which usually go up steadily over the years. Fees that are affordable today may be prohibitive 10 years from now.

Some retirees decide to buy houses or condos in a warmer climate. Mr. Kerr suggests strongly that people rent for a few months first, citing the case of a retired pilot and his wife who sold their house in Canada and moved to Arizona. It took them only three months to get their fill of the hot blazing sun, endless golf games and older neighbours with different interests. They quickly sold their Arizona house and returned to Canada.

Canadians owning real estate in the United States may feel the impact of U.S. estate tax, though not as badly as before. The U.S. Internal Revenue Service used to tax non-residents after death if they had U.S. property worth more than $60,000 (U.S.) in value. But Canadians who lived full-time in the sun belt were considered U.S. residents and their estate tax exemption was a much higher $600,000. This inequity has been recognized in recent revisions to the Canada-U.S. tax treaty, which will have retroactive application. Once those revisions are ratified by the two governments, those who paid the excess tax can claim it back retroactively.

There are ways to lessen the estate tax bite, so anyone with substantial assets in the United States should get advice. Look for an accountant or qualified financial planner in Canada who is familiar with U.S. tax law. There may be questions that come up at the same time, such as when snowbirds have to file a U.S. tax return and pay U.S. income tax, or how long they can stay in the United States without losing their Canadian medical care coverage.

A final point of interest to snowbirds. There is no need to change your will just because you are spending time in the United States, says Mr. Kerr, even if there's a chance you will die there. The Canadian will is valid in the United States, though it may have to go through probate in the state where you have property as well as in Canada. Sometimes, the U.S. probating can be avoided by showing the authorities the probate documents from Canada.

When Parents Need Care

People are staying healthy and fit longer than ever before, and of course that's what we all wish for our own parents. But sometimes, they reach a point in the aging process (as my in-laws did) where they can no longer manage on their own. That's when children have to make some tough decisions, along with the parents if possible, about what comes next.

Today, many resources in the community help the elderly remain at home. The idea of "aging in place" is becoming popular with governments as a way to shrink bloated health care budgets. You will find a wealth of public and private services that provide home care, health aids and communication links to seniors living alone.

But there may come a time when your parents are better off moving to a retirement community or senior citizens' complex, where they can get nutritious meals and 24-hour-a-day help. There are many types of long-term care facilities and, as Ann Rhodes notes in *The Eldercare Sourcebook*, the names are different in each province. You can get a headache sorting through the lodges, manors, homes for the aged and continuing care retirement communities, trying to decide whether they are private, non-profit, government-operated or government-subsidized.

Where do you start your search? Ms. Rhodes suggests several sources of information on what she calls alternative accommodation:

- Staff at public libraries can direct you to listings of homes. Many libraries have two comprehensive guides, *Directory of Long-Term Care Centres in Canada* and *Canadian Hospital Directory*. Both are published by the Canadian Hospital Association and updated regularly.

- The provincial housing ministry may have a registry of retirement homes and lodges. It may also participate in providing low-cost housing for the elderly.
- Contact the local office of Canada Mortgage and Housing. Sometimes, CMHC teams up with other authorities to provide low-cost housing for elders.
- Look in the Yellow Pages under "Retirement Communities and Homes."

To cut down the legwork, look for a social worker or public health nurse who knows the facilities in the area and can help you decide what would suit your parents. A local family service association is a good source of referrals, as is the Victorian Order of Nurses. In some provinces, there is a single agency or entry point for elder care assessment and placement.

Your employer can also help. Many large companies have an employee assistance program, with counselling and referrals for elder care. Consult your family doctor, your parents' doctors or, if your parents have been hospitalized, the hospital's discharge coordinator. Obviously, the search is more complicated if you live far away from your parents and can make only occasional visits.

When checking out a facility, there's no substitute for making personal visits and speaking with staff and residents. The first sight of frail elderly people en masse can be quite a shock. "You'll see people asleep in chairs, heads back, mouths open.You'll see the cognitively impaired wandering around aimlessly," says Michelle West in *Seniority: In Search of the Best Nursing Homes and Alternative Care in Canada*. "Residents may be wearing mismatched shoes or clothes inside out, sights that must not be assumed to be a reflection of the care these people are receiving."

To know what questions to ask when you inspect a facility, order "Nursing Home Checklist," a nine-page pamphlet published by an Ontario consumer advocacy group. It's available for $5 (to cover postage and handling) from Concerned Friends of Ontario Citizens in Care Facilities, P.O. Box 1054, Station Q, Toronto, Ont. M4T 2P2.

Long-term care is very expensive. Room and board in a privately owned retirement facility can easily cost $3,000 to $4,000 a month. At that rate, elderly parents will run through their savings quickly—and so will you if you are supporting them. But many government-owned and non-profit facilities accept patients who have no savings and can hand over only their monthly pensions.

Now here's a sensitive issue. Your parents may have assets, but they prefer to leave them in their estate and not deplete them in long-term care. A financial planner can help your parents transfer these assets to children, grandchildren or a trust, so they qualify for government subsidies. Don't make any moves without professional advice, however, because this is complex stuff and will have tax and estate consequences.

Parents as Dependents

Whether your parents are in long-term care or living at home, you can get some tax breaks if they depend on you for financial support. Revenue Canada provides several tax credits for older people, which can be transferred to younger family members who support them.

- You may claim a parent as a dependent for tax purposes. He or she does not have to live under your roof, but must be living in Canada at some time during the year and must be mentally or physically infirm. In 1993, you could claim a federal tax credit of $269, as long as the dependent's income did not exceed $2,690. The credit was reduced to zero if the dependent's income was $4,273 or more.

  The low-income limit rules out anyone over 65 who gets the old age pension. (The maximum benefit under

Old Age Security was $4,586 in 1993.) However, not everyone qualifies for the full pension. If they have not lived in Canada for 10 years immediately before applying, their pension is reduced. But many low-income pensioners also receive the Guaranteed Income Supplement, worth up to $5,450 in 1993 for a single person, and more if there are spousal benefits.

- You can claim a parent's medical expenses if he or she lives in Canada and depends on you for financial support. But you have to reduce the expenses claimed if the parent's income is more than a certain amount ($6,456 in 1993). To generate any tax savings, your total medical expenses (including a spouse and dependents) must be more than 3 per cent of net income or above a certain dollar amount ($1,614 in 1993).

  There is a long list of eligible medical expenses, and you can find examples in the annual tax guide. (Call Revenue Canada if you need more details.) They include payments for prescription drugs, eyeglasses, hearing aids, wheelchairs, premiums paid to private health care plans, nurses, doctors and dentists. Also, you can claim the cost of modifying your home to accommodate a parent with impaired mobility.

- You can claim the unused part of a parent's disability credit if he or she lives with you. The federal credit, worth $720 in 1993, is available to those who have a severe mental or physical impairment that restricts their ability to perform basic activities of daily living. This is explained in Revenue Canada's booklet "Tax Information for People with Disabilities."

  To get the disability credit, your parent must have a medical certificate from a doctor or optometrist. (The cost is not covered by provincial medicare plans.) Also, the impairment must have lasted or be expected to last for at least a year. A person who claims the cost of a full-time attendant or full-time care in a nursing home as a medical expense cannot claim the disability credit too. One or the other, but not both.

Making Funeral Arrangements

As your parents get older, they will spend more and more of their time going to funerals for friends and family. When they tell you about ceremonies they have attended, they will probably give their opinions on what they like and dislike and what they want for themselves. This is a perfect opportunity for you to introduce the subject of their own funeral arrangements and to offer to help in whatever way you can.

You may get an opening for a conversation when a celebrity dies and there is publicity about the funeral arrangements. Or if you have made your own plans for what you want when you die, you can describe them to your parents and break the ice that way. Often when people get ill, they grow anxious to talk about the subject themselves.

We all have heard horror stories about greedy undertakers preying on grief-stricken families and selling them overpriced coffins and bereavement services. That's why it makes sense to preplan your funeral—or at least leave instructions about the rites of passage you prefer. Many people also make sure there is enough money to pay for the funeral costs so survivors don't have to dip into their own pockets.

"Arranging a funeral is too important to be left to the last minute," says consumer advocate Donald Flynn. "If you understand that you have alternatives, and if you can thoroughly discuss them with your family or friends, you can save hundreds of dollars and untold worry and grief." Mr. Flynn, a second-generation funeral director with 25 years of experience, gives helpful tips on how to shop for funerals, cremation and cemetery plots in his self-published book, *The Truth about Funerals*.

People who prefer a simple, no-frills funeral service should talk it over with their families in advance, he advises. Survivors are often upset, even outraged, when a loved one chooses a stark "disposal service," as the funeral industry calls it. Spouses, partners and children should be consulted, because funerals are also for the living, to help them confront their grief and start putting it behind them.

When people choose a funeral, there are four main areas of conflict for families:

- Is the person buried or cremated?
- Is there a traditional funeral ceremony, a memorial service with no casket or a scattering of the cremated ashes?
- Is the casket open or closed?
- Does the family receive visitors at the funeral home?

Cover all the bases with your parents and see if they are open to input. Suggest that if they refuse to discuss their plans in detail and simply leave written instructions in a will, they are shutting you out. This can cause future problems, possibly hurting their chances of having their wishes followed.

The executor certainly should be involved in the funeral plans, and depending on your parents' preferences, a clergy member can be helpful. But in order to avoid pressure to overspend, Mr. Flynn cautions against talking to a funeral home in the consultation phase. The goal for consumers: "When you meet face-to-face with the funeral director, you are better informed than he expects you to be."

If your parents want to leave money to cover the funeral costs, they can do it through a life insurance policy. The insurance proceeds are tax-free and paid a short time after death, without having to wait for the will to be probated. But life insurance should be bought early in life. It can be prohibitively expensive for older people or, if there is a medical condition, not available at all.

Most of us have seen ads on late-night television offering guaranteed insurance for older people, regardless of their health. They play on a person's fear of leaving unpaid debts behind. The problem with these policies is that, despite their low price, they provide very little coverage and contain many exclusions.

"Even at 'pennies a day,' most of these policies are atrocious buys," says *Consumer Reports* magazine, which bought a number of them and scrutinized the fine print in its November 1993 issue. For an annual outlay of $240 to $360, a man in his early sixties or a woman in her late sixties gets about $3,000 to $5,000 worth of coverage. That's precious little to cover burial costs and other outstanding claims on a person's estate.

Furthermore, these policies pay reduced benefits if a person dies of natural causes in the first two years. Insurers do this to protect themselves from people in bad health who buy insurance and die shortly afterwards. But the death benefits in the early years barely exceed the annual premiums.

Take the guaranteed life insurance plan offered by Norwich Union Life of Toronto, which offers a choice of five monthly premiums ranging from $20 to $75. If a 65-year-old man chooses to pay $30 a month, his death benefit is $4,600. But if he dies within the first two years—say after 20 months—his beneficiary receives only one-and-a-half times the $600 in premiums he paid before his death, a total of $900.

The benefits are higher if the policyholder dies in an accident. The man in our example will leave $2,700 to his beneficiary if his death after 20 months is accidental. And if he dies any time after two years in an accident, his death benefit is tripled to $13,800. But accidental death is rare among people over 60—about one death in ten. "We consider low-value life insurance policies sold to the elderly to be a disgrace," concludes *Consumer Reports*, arguing that they should be improved or banned.

Many retirees have no life insurance at all, other than what an employer provides through group benefits. (These policies can be extended after an employee leaves the company, though often with reduced coverage.) An older husband may decide he doesn't need any life insurance, especially if his children are grown and he has no dependents other than his wife. He may already have provided for his spouse to receive the bulk of his estate and to be covered by his company and other pensions once he dies.

Also, there is a death benefit to subsidize funeral costs under the Canada Pension Plan. (An estimated 20 per cent of those eligible don't know about the benefit.) The amount is calculated on the number of years the deceased paid into CPP and his or her income; the maximum in 1994 was $3,400. The executor normally applies, but if there's no estate, the surviving spouse or next of kin should apply. Forms are available from funeral homes, insurance companies, social agencies and government offices.

Funeral directors often suggest to older people that they pay for the funeral ahead of time. They argue that prepayment guarantees that all costs will be covered and there will be no additional charges to the family. Not true, says Mr. Flynn. Funeral homes can bill extra for services rendered at the time of death but not covered in the itemized contract. Also, any changes or substitutions may nullify the contract.

To prepay funeral costs, people are better off putting the money in a savings account rather than leaving it with a funeral home, he argues. It's safer and transferable when you control it. However, there is a tax advantage with a prepaid funeral plan because interest earned each year is not taxable up to a $15,000 limit. Interest on a savings account is taxable.

Another problem with prepaid plans is that funeral homes can be sold or go into receivership, and trust accounts can be administered by unscrupulous people. If your parents insist on prepaying their funeral costs—perhaps they want to tie up loose ends and get everything settled—they should read the contract carefully. Among the things to watch for: What interest will be paid? How much will they lose if they have a cash crunch and cancel the contract or make partial cash withdrawals? If they move far away in the future, can they transfer the contract to a new funeral home? Will they get to choose which funeral home?

In any case, it is possible to prearrange a funeral without paying for it in advance. Most funeral directors will provide a complete price list and a contract that spells out all the details. They don't have to guarantee the prices, but their written quotation will be handy for future reference.

You and your parents may want to join a memorial society. This is a non-profit volunteer organization that helps members plan, and negotiate with cooperating funeral homes, for less expensive and more modest arrangements. To find a local memorial society, contact the Memorial Society Association of Canada, P.O. Box 96, Station A, Weston, Ont. M9N 3M6, telephone (416) 241-6274.

Dealing with an Inheritance

The past few years have seen a flood of articles about the "trillion-dollar windfall." This refers to the amount of money Canada's baby boomers stand to inherit from their parents. The older generation picked up frugal habits after scraping through the lean years of the Great Depression and the Second World War, and in several decades of postwar prosperity they amassed a vast pool of assets. With mortgages long since paid off, many of these people are living in houses bought in the 1950s for less than $20,000 and now worth sometimes more than $300,000.

Unless Canadian politicians bring back inheritance taxes—and there are moves afoot to do so—very little of this huge transfer of wealth between generations will end up in government hands. A good chunk will be lost to capital gains tax, which will hit more estates than before with the elimination of the $100,000 capital gains exemption in February 1994. But with astute advice and estate planning, elderly parents can pass on the bulk of their money tax-free to children, grandchildren and possibly great grandchildren.

The potential wild card is how much these cautious savers plan to spend on themselves in retirement. Will they sell their mortgage-free houses and liquidate their stocks and bonds, using the cash to indulge themselves during their declining years? In Florida, at many retirement communities, residents wear T-shirts proclaiming, "We're spending our kids' inheritance."

Or will a longer life expectancy, coupled with higher health care costs and a fraying government safety net, deplete their assets? Life expectancy tables indicate that a 70-year-old man will survive till the age of 83 and a 70-year-old woman will live to 85. (My in-laws have already beaten the averages.) The longer parents live, the smaller the estate they will likely leave to their heirs.

It is imprudent to count on an inheritance to bail you out of financial difficulties, warns Michael Nuschke, a Halifax financial planner who, like me, is skeptical of stories about a trillion-dollar windfall that may never materialize. Baby boomers caught in the sandwich between needy elderly parents and financially dependent children may be squeezed in another way, he says: "They may find themselves taking more sandwiches to work."

So, you shouldn't take anything for granted. One study of elderly people in retirement communities found a large number leaving their money to older friends they meet in their later years. Parents who remarry may leave their assets to a much younger spouse, or split their property between children and stepchildren. And homeowners who need an income may sign up for a reverse mortgage and lose all the home equity they built up over the years.

Of course, many boomers will come into money while their parents are still alive. If Mom and Dad could afford it, they probably helped you buy your first house. Now they're contributing to a college fund for your children. They may also step in with financial support if you lose your job or want to start your own business.

But one day—and you hope it doesn't come too soon—you may find yourself with a sizable bequest left to you in a parent's will. If so, how will you handle it? You and your spouse may face a tangle of conflicting goals—paying off your mortgage, helping your children buy their first home, taking a sabbatical or around-the-world trip, giving money to charity or putting it all in the bank.

Inherited wealth can be a burden as well as a pleasure. Some people become obsessed with safeguarding the money, resenting the smallest expenditure and suspecting the motives of those close to them. Others worry that their parents didn't enjoy the money and wonder if they can avoid making the same mistakes.

When you inherit money, the whole world will be your friend. So the best advice is to wait before making any investments. "Although you shouldn't allow your new wealth to make you paranoid and suspicious," says *New York Times* personal finance columnist Mary Rowland, "it doesn't pay to be overly trusting of those who offer to manage it for you either." Earning a modest return on the money for a while—even a year—will be better in the long run than making a big mistake and losing a lot up front.

Put off major life decisions, such as selling your house or changing your job, during the first year. Go out and buy something nice, then sit back and spend some time thinking about how you will manage the rest. Move slowly and don't invest all the money at once. Spread your money among several investments, not just one.

At some point, you may want to find a trustworthy financial advisor to help you invest the money and sort out your financial priorities. Start by talking to your parents' advisors and see if you feel comfortable with them. At the very least, they will give you an idea of how the money was invested before, so you can carry on in the same style if you want.

Financial Planners and Investment Counsellors

If you want independent advice, consult a financial planner. Financial planners are generalists: they have a good basic knowledge of investing, taxes, family law, insurance and estate planning, and can refer you to a specialist if you need more detailed advice. Ask the planner to project how much income you will receive from your inherited capital, assuming different rates of tax, interest, inflation and stock returns.

Another question to ask a financial planner is whether you are better off investing the inheritance or using it to pay off outstanding debts, such as the mortgage on your house. In general, eliminating debt is a far better investment than holding stocks, bonds or guaranteed investment certificates. That's because investment income is taxed at a high marginal rate, whereas loan payments are made in after-tax dollars. If you are in a 50 per cent tax bracket, paying off a car loan at 9 per cent is about the same as earning an 18 per cent pre-tax return on an investment—and mighty few investments pay that much.

But at the same time, a good financial planner will point out the danger of using inherited money to pay off a mortgage. Under the law in many provinces, an inheritance does not have to be shared when a couple separates or divorces, but a family home must be shared. So if one spouse uses inherited cash to pay down a mortgage on the family home, he or she will lose some of it if the marriage subsequently breaks down.

I said a *good* financial planner will alert you to this possible trap. But how do you find one? People who call themselves financial planners are not regulated by government, except in Quebec and Alberta, so the quality ranges all over the map. When interviewing advisors, ask if they have taken courses and qualified for a recognized designation such as

Chartered Financial Planner (C.F.P.), Registered Financial Planner (R.F.P.) or Chartered Financial Consultant (Ch. F.C.). Ask also if they belong to the Canadian Association of Financial Planners, a voluntary industry group that sponsors a code of ethics and continuing education programs.

If you want a copy of the CAFP's code of ethics, along with a brochure explaining how financial planning works and a directory of members in your area, contact the Canadian Association of Financial Planners, 60 St. Clair Ave. East, Suite 510, Toronto, Ont. M4T 1N5, telephone (416) 966-9928.

An issue when hiring a financial planner is how they are paid. Usually, you pay a commission, based on whatever investment products you buy. Less commonly, you are charged a fee, either a flat price or an hourly rate. Sometimes, you pay both a fee and a commission. Fee-only planners say they can be more objective because they have no financial stake in purchases they recommend. Commission-based planners say they give unbiased advice to middle-income clients who can't afford to pay fees. You have to decide what makes you feel more comfortable, but it's crucial that the financial planner's method of compensation is disclosed to you.

Stockbrokers also earn income from commissions and they, too, can be subject to conflicts of interest. Clients sometimes complain that a broker actively traded, or "churned," their account to make more money, or favoured stocks that the employer firm had underwritten. If you are hiring a broker, look for someone with at least five to ten years of experience—enough to have experienced at least one stock market downturn—and upgraded credentials. Check for the initials F.C.S.I. (Fellow of the Canadian Securities Institute) or C.I.M. (Canadian Investment Management), which shows the broker has completed extra courses.

When you have a significant amount of money to invest, say $250,000 to $1 million, you may want to hire an investment counsellor. These people have all the qualifications of a stockbroker and more, and they manage money on a discretionary basis. This means you don't make any trading decisions and they make them all for you. Are you comfortable with this type of arrangement? You will pay an investment counsellor an annual fee, based on the value of your portfolio. Typical fees are 1 to 1.5 per cent, paid quarterly, and they are tax-deductible.

To compete with investment counsellors, some brokerage firms offer fee-based accounts, or "wrap accounts." A stockbroker will assess your requirements and match you up with independent investment counsellors, then monitor the results. (Rarely do clients speak directly to the money manager.) Fees range from 2.5 to 3 per cent and they are tax-deductible.

A fee-based manager has a vested interest in making your money grow. The more you earn, the more he or she earns too. If you have a $200,000 portfolio and pay a 2 per cent annual fee, the manager will earn $4,000. But if your assets grow to be worth $300,000, then the manager's compensation will swell to $6,000.

A good source of advice on investment counsellors and wrap accounts is *The Insider's Guide to Choosing the Best Money Manager*, by Kelly Rodgers, a chartered financial analyst, who has worked as an investment counsellor.

Trust Companies

If your parents have named a trust company as executor and if estate assets remain in a trust, the money will be invested and managed by trust company staff. Dealing with them may leave you angry and frustrated, since trust companies are known for making conservative—some say stodgy—investment decisions. In most provinces, trust companies are bound by laws limiting the portion of a portfolio they can invest in stocks. Often, they are prohibited from investing in mutual funds. So, at a time when stocks and equity funds are going gangbusters (as they were in 1993), the bulk of your money will be sitting in low-interest investments.

Many people often complain about the administration of family money by trust companies. What makes them even madder is that trusts cannot easily be moved from one institution to another. After citing a litany of overdrafts, increasing charges and sloppiness, one person said, "How can a trust company get away with this? I fear I know the answer—I can't remove the account. But is there no control on such practices?" Another irate heir castigated a trust company for highhanded service, numerous errors and stiff fees for all manner of services, including preparing tax slips: "On my father's modest estate of less than $500,000, the trust company has charged and accrued fees in excess of $51,000, with more to come."

Acting as Trustee

When your parents die, you may be called upon to play a role other than inheritor. Instead of leaving money to you, they may skip a generation and create a trust for their grandchildren, making you the trustee. You would be given the power to determine which of the grandchildren get the money, when they get it and for what purposes. The trust could be set up to ensure the grandchildren don't get the capital until they are fairly old. Or it could pass the capital to the greatgrandchildren, says Ottawa tax lawyer Arthur Drache. "Trusts are almost infinitely flexible if they are drawn up by people who know what they are doing."

Coming into a sizable amount of money can be traumatic, particularly when it is accompanied by the death of a parent—a watershed event in many people's lives. Often, you don't feel good about the inheritance because of the way you got it. So don't rush. Put the money in the bank for a while, so your sense of loss and other strong emotions don't colour your decision-making.

If you feel guilty about inheriting money and wonder whether you really deserve it, relax. It's a common response. You have just taken possession of the culmination of your parent's lifelong financial struggle. Naturally, you feel ambivalent and unsure of what to do. But with time and astute advice, you can choose the option that is right for you—either spending it on yourself and your family or acting as a responsible steward to make the money grow and preserve it for future generations.

5 RAISING A FAMILY

Having children may be one of the greatest joys you will ever experience, but remember: children are expensive and entail a major adjustment in your life, both financial and emotional. There are both the out-of-pocket costs and the opportunity costs, the chances for economic betterment you lose because of the presence of children.

Women bear the brunt of childrearing and usually give up more in income, pensions and career advancement. Yet both partners make sacrifices when babies are born. Travel is no longer as easy or as carefree. There is less money for saving, eating out and spending on yourself. And, of course, there is a time crunch that hits you without warning in the first moments of infancy and doesn't really let up until the last pangs of adolescence.

In today's uncertain economy, many couples are limiting themselves to one or two children to avoid taking on more than they can afford. It can cost $150,000 or more to raise a child to age 18, according to Manitoba's Agriculture Ministry. By far the biggest expense in the early years is child care. Then comes food, clothing, housing and health care. Boys eat more, especially when they reach their teens, while girls cost more to clothe.

One consolation: costs are higher for the first child. Furniture and clothes can be reused and the same caregiver can look after several children at a time. Nevertheless, a large family can really put a squeeze on family finances. Parents have to devote more time to their jobs to bring home bigger paycheques or cut back on their own spending.

Married couples with children spend more on just about everything than couples without children, according to the Vanier Institute of the Family in its 1994 publication *Profiling Canada's Families*. In only one category are childless couples ahead—savings. Unfortunately, saving money takes a back seat to the immediate costs of raising children.

The average middle-income, dual-earner family that owns a home and has one child spends about 15 per cent of its gross income to feed, clothe, house, educate and care for its offspring. A family with two kids spends almost a quarter of its before-tax income. And with three or more kids, a family invests almost a third of its income in child-rearing costs.

Raising children invariably costs more than parents anticipate and forces more changes in our lives than we're prepared to admit. Here are some of the big financial adjustments we make in the early years. (I have excluded saving for education, which is covered in chapter 6.)

Hiring Child Care

If you take time off from work when your baby is born or when you've adopted a baby, then go back either part-time or full-time, you have to pay for child care—unless there is a helpful family member who can babysit for free. Your main choices are an organized day care centre, a babysitter or nanny living in your house or living out, or home-based care in the neighbourhood.

In our 13 years of parenthood, we have tried all the options. When Charles was a baby, he was looked after from noon to six by a stay-at-home mother on our block with two older boys. He enjoyed being with other kids and joining in family mealtimes, and we liked the convenience of taking him across the street, although we didn't have the luxury of a later pickup time if things got frantic at work. When Charles was two, we hired a live-out nanny. This made life easier because we could leave earlier or come back later and have someone do the housework while we were away. We still have a part-time nanny, who works from two till seven and some evenings. Richard spent two years at a day care program while he attended an afternoon kindergarten class.

My experience has taught me that there is no best child care arrangement for all parents. You look for whatever suits you and your child at the time and try to stay flexible, because things change. For most families, finding high-quality, reliable and affordable long-term care is a struggle.

Regulated child care, either in day care centres or family day care homes, is preferred by many parents, but generally not available. In 1991, there were 2.2 million Canadian children 12 or younger who required care for at least 20 hours a week while their parents worked or studied. Yet with an estimated 333,000 regulated child care spaces, only 15 per cent of these children could be served by licensed care arrangements.

Some families arrange their work schedules so one parent is available for child care while the other is working. One in six dual-earner couples deliberately shifted work hours in 1988, according to a national child care study. Two-thirds of parents who did this said their primary reason was they considered it best for the child, while one-third said they chose this option to reduce child care costs.

How can you save money on child care? Live-in help generally costs less than live-out, because you can deduct room and board from the employee's paycheque. However, you may have to convert your basement into nanny quarters or install a separate apartment in your house. You and the nanny will be uncomfortable living too close together.

You can also save by hiring a nanny from overseas who may have less experience and lower wage demands than someone already living in Canada. But be prepared to wait six months or longer. Because of high unemployment, the federal government has tightened the rules and made it harder to sponsor nannies from outside the country.

A growing number of working parents are cutting costs by sharing care, with one babysitter tending to children from several families in one of the couple's homes. This arrangement can provide big savings and give your child the benefit of socializing with other kids. As long as everyone gets along—and that's a big if—it's a good solution.

One way to make child care more affordable is to quit your full-time job and work freelance at home while continuing to hire a part-time or full-time nanny. If you can do the same work in a home office or start a home-based sales or consulting business, you will find the gross salary you need to earn is significantly less because of the tax deductions available to self-employed workers. Toronto financial planner Janet Freedman estimates that a parent needs to make only $20,000 gross annually at home to net the same amount as a salaried employee grossing $35,000. That $15,000 differential includes lower child care costs for parents working at home.

If your take-home pay covers nothing more than child care and commuting, you may be tempted to quit and stay home with the baby. But even if the economics don't seem to add up, you are probably better off staying in the work force. Think of it as an investment in your future earning power. Eventually, your child care costs will drop and your income will go up and there will be a clear financial benefit. Meanwhile, if you take a long sabbatical from paid work, your skills may get rusty and you may not command the same kind of salary when you are ready to go back in. And given the harsh reality of layoffs, divorce and widowhood, it is risky to depend on your mate as the sole wage earner.

Working part-time has advantages. You will probably pay less tax when the second income is reduced, because you fall into a lower tax bracket. Child care costs are cut and benefits given up by the part-timer may still be covered by the other partner. You won't lose your skills, work contacts and confidence, nor will you have to endure the harsh re-entry challenges that a stay-at-home parent eventually faces.

Remember that the government is your partner in paying for babysitting or day care, since child care expenses are tax-deductible within certain limits. Here are the rules:

- Common-law couples of the opposite sex are treated the same as married couples for purposes of calculating child care expenses if they have had a child together or they have lived together in a conjugal relationship for at least 12 continuous months.
- You can claim child care expenses if you or your spouse needed help looking after your kids in order to work, carry on a business, take an occupational training course or do grant-funded research.
- You can deduct up to $5,000 for each child under seven at the end of the year and up to $3,000 for each child under 14 at any time during the year. A child who is severely disabled and dependent is eligible for the $5,000 deduction at any age.
- If you are self-employed, you are limited to the $3,000 and $5,000 deductions. You cannot claim child care expenses as business expenses.
- Eligible expenses include day care or babysitting, nursery school, boarding school and camp. Payments to a boarding school or camp are limited to $150 a week for children under seven and $90 a week for children from seven to 14.

- The deduction is limited to two-thirds of earned income and must be claimed by the lower-income spouse. The exception is Quebec, where either spouse can claim the deduction; it is limited to the full earned income of the lower-income spouse.
- The deduction is based on when the services are provided, rather than on when the amounts are paid. "So prepaying in December does not give you the deduction a year earlier," says accounting firm KPMG Peat Marwick Thorne in *The Canadian Personal Tax Planning Guide*.
- You need receipts for child care expenses, though you don't have to submit them with your tax return (except in Quebec). Some caregivers prefer not to give receipts, because they don't want to claim the income and pay tax on it. But it is safer to deal with a caregiver who provides receipts. If you are ever audited, you will have something on paper to back up your expense claims. You also need the caregiver's address and social insurance number.

As most working parents know, the cost of child care usually exceeds the amount you can write off on your income tax. The maximums have not kept pace with inflation and are adjusted only occasionally. A live-out nanny in an urban area grosses about $15,000 to $20,000 a year, including taxes. But parents with two children are allowed to deduct only $6,000 to $10,000 a year, depending on the age of their kids.

When hiring a full-time babysitter or nanny, make sure you keep detailed records. As an employer, you have to pay for your employee's health care plan, workers' compensation, income tax, Canada Pension Plan and unemployment insurance. Unless you are organized, you'll spend hours on paperwork and face stiff penalties if your remittances arrive late.

You have to file a minimum of 12 forms a year for employee taxes and benefits, plus an annual accounting in February. Whether you are General Motors or an individual hiring a nanny for the first time, the tax filing requirements are the same. So, prepare to spend a few minutes a month filling out government forms. It's a hassle, but very costly if you miss the deadlines.

As your children get older, finding suitable care becomes less of a drain on your time and resources. Once they start going to school, you can get by with after-school care from neighbours, local teenagers or a part-time babysitter. And some schools provide child care for working parents. Eventually, the older children can look after their younger siblings, at least some of the time.

Meanwhile, you can continue to deduct up to $3,000 a year in expenses for each child under 14. If they don't need care during the school year, you can use the deduction for day camps during school breaks or summer camps. However, your claim for camps is limited to $90 a week for older children, probably quite a bit less than what you will actually pay.

Adopting a Child

Biological parents have greater access to parenthood than adoptive parents do. They can have children at will and conceive any number of children they like. Age is no barrier as long as the parents are fertile, nor is poor health or disability, low income or an unorthodox lifestyle. Singles, common-law and same-sex couples can all reproduce.

Adoptive parents, however, face barriers to parenthood. If they already have one child, they may find some placements are available only to childless adopters. Prospective parents seen as too young or too old or with too large a gap between their ages may be denied a chance to adopt; similar restrictions may apply to unwell or disabled adopters. And unorthodox couples often face legal obstacles to adoption. Many provinces prohibit the partner of a gay parent from adopting the parent's child, even if they are living in a long-term relationship. If the biological parent dies or becomes disabled, the surviving partner has no right to care for the child, even if that would be in the child's best interest. The result is disruption and family breakup.

All adoptions require a cash outlay, says Nancy Thalia Reynolds in *Adopting Your Child: Options, Answers and Actions.* Subsidies exist, but coverage for all expenses is rare. Complex legal and agency systems can be intimidating, and assumptions about fitness to parent may favour middle-class adopters at the expense of poor adopters.

Moreover, the expenses are seldom known in advance. If the adoption fails, the fees may not be waived. Insurance against some failed adoptions exists, but costs thousands of dollars. Adoption fees are not tax-deductible. And a few unfortunate adopters are victims of fraud, paying large fees without receiving a child.

"The consumer movement has been around for 30 years and yet it seems scarcely to have touched the world of adoption," says Ms. Reynolds, who with her husband has a biological son and a daughter adopted privately from Brazil. "Yet businesses, government agencies, non-profit corporations and professionals specializing in adoption are as likely as any others to be of high or low quality, efficient or disorganized, overpriced or a bargain, ethical or unprincipled."

She advises parents to budget for possible fee hikes when planning an adoption. Those adopting internationally will find that costs are market-driven and less subject to legal and social controls than at home. (A comprehensive report, *Adoption in Canada*, found there were three international adoptions for every two domestic adoptions in Canada in 1991.) Some agency adoptions take years to come through and an agency may not ask you to pay a placement fee until the child is referred to you. After agreeing to a fee in writing, find out if you will be expected to cover a further increase.

Adoptive parents in Canada have a statutory right to take time off work when a child arrives, just as biological parents do. However, getting enough time off may be difficult if you are adopting internationally. It may be necessary to take several trips, usually several months apart, without knowing in advance how long you will have to stay. Be frank with your employer: give advance notice so your absence will be covered and negotiate for a flexible adoption leave.

About 60 per cent of adoptions are by stepparents, says Ms. Reynolds: "Stepparent adoption can be well worth pursuing, especially where ties with the non-custodial parent are loose or nonexistent, because it will give the stepparent legal parental rights should their spouse become incapacitated or die." But the biological parent usually has to consent for the adoption to take place, and stepchildren above a certain age must consent too. If adoption is problematic because a necessary consent isn't given, stepparents can review other legal alternatives, such as custody or guardianship.

Choosing Summer Camps

Unless you have a second home in the country, you will have to find activities to keep the kids busy in the summer. Few children thrive with nothing to do for the entire nine or ten weeks that school is out. The younger they are, the more they need a structured program. There are all kinds of day camps to choose from. In the past decade, there has been a proliferation of specialty camps. You can find camps devoted to every conceivable sport, as well as for computers, chess, mathematics, music, drama, business and even circus skills. There are also camps for children with special needs and health problems.

But day camp can be expensive, and overnight camp is even more of a big-ticket item. Parents can easily spend $150 to $250 a week for day camp in the city and up to $500 a week for overnight camp. If you send several kids to camp, you have to save up money ahead or face a big hole in your budget. There are some free programs around, but they fill up quickly and you can't be sure of getting a space.

To find a suitable camp, get recommendations from friends and neighbours, or by calling your local parks and recreation department, school or community centre. Once you have narrowed down your choices, you have to do some research and ask some questions. Here is a checklist, provided by the Ontario Camping Association:

- What is the ratio of counsellors to campers? A good rule of thumb is one to seven for children under eight years of age, and one to ten for older children. Children with special needs may require a one-to-one ratio.
- How old are the counsellors? The OCA suggests they should be at least 17, although many day camp counsellors are younger.
- How are the staff hired and checked? Do they have training in first aid and lifesaving, and experience in camping and working with children?
- What is the camp's philosophy? This is an important aspect of the camp, which underlies its activities. If the brochures don't say anything, call the camp director and ask about it.
- What is the camp director's background? How long has he or she been running the same camp?
- What percentage of campers return each year? Has the staff been working there for several seasons?
- Is the camp willing to provide names of parents to call for references?
- What kind of transportation is provided? If schoolbuses are used, find out how large they are and what safety features they have. Who will be driving the buses? Is staff on board to watch and control the kids?

- Will the children be picked up and dropped off at your house or at a central location?
- If children are taken off-site for outings, how are they supervised? A one-to-ten ratio of counsellors to campers may not be adequate for outings and extra supervision may be required.
- Is there an "early bird" special for people who register and pay early?

Parents looking for a camp program may wish to contact the Canadian Camping Association, a national organization linking camps in all provinces, at 1806 Avenue Rd., Suite 2, Toronto, Ont. M5M 3Z1, telephone (416) 781-4717. There are also provincial associations that offer general information and an annual list of member camps. Camps accredited by the provincial associations meet specific standards in health, safety, food preparation, accommodations, programs, staffing, maintenance, transportation and administration. If a camp director says the camp is not accredited, parents should ask why not.

British Columbia Camping Association, c/o Thunderbird Outdoor Centre, 880 Courtney St., Victoria, B.C. V8W 1C4; (604) 386-7511.

Alberta Camping Association, Percy Page Centre, 11759 Groat Rd., Edmonton, Alta. T5M 3K6; (403) 453-8570.

Saskatchewan Camping Association, c/o Saskatchewan YMCA, 25–22nd St. East, Saskatoon, Sask. S7K 0C7; (306) 652-7515.

Manitoba Camping Association, 194-A Sherbrook St., Winnipeg, Man. R3C 2B6; (204) 784-1134.

Ontario Camping Association, 1806 Avenue Rd., Suite 2, Toronto, Ont. M5M 3Z1; (416) 781-0525.

Association des Camps du Québec, 4545 ave. Pierre de Coubertin, C. P. 1000, Succursale M, Montreal, Que. H1V 3R2; (514) 252-3113.

New Brunswick Camping Association, Regent Station, 4–403 Regent St., Fredericton, N.B. E3B 3X6; (506) 459-1929.

Camping Association of Nova Scotia, Box 3243 S, Halifax, N.S. B3J 3H5; (902) 865-3523.

Newfoundland and Labrador Camping Association, Box 760, Bishop's Falls, Nfld. A0H 1C0; (709) 258-5862.

Planning a Family Vacation

Taking kids on vacation can be an enjoyable family time. It can also be horrible. Your success depends on how much planning went into the trip and how well your children adapt to strange surroundings and an unfamiliar routine. If the holiday goes well, you can be spontaneous and self-indulgent, curious and adventurous, and get to know each other better. If it goes badly, you curse your kids as they bicker, whine and complain, and count the minutes till you head home and back to work. Taking trips with babies is a logistical challenge and teenagers are usually happier staying home or taking separate vacations.

Every family is different. Some like to rough it, sleeping under the stars and cooking all their own food. Others (like our gang) prefer the comfort of hotels and restaurant meals. And everyone has a favourite destination. But no matter where you go, say Dorothy Jordon and Marjorie Adoff Cohen in *Great Vacations with Your Kids,* there are six keys to a great family holiday:

- Plan your vacation with the individual needs of each family member in mind. Start with the youngest child and work your way up. Work on all the details ahead of time. Be sure there are cribs or roll-out cots, find out if there is a children's program, ask if you can warm the baby's bottle on the plane and so on.
- Include every member of the family in the planning. The kids should be actively involved from the beginning. Since change and new places can be upsetting to

them, they will be more accommodating if some of the unknowns are eliminated. Let them know ahead of time where you are going and what you are doing and let them participate in the decision-making.

- Make sure there is time to be apart as well as together. Spend every minute together and you'll go crazy. You don't do it at home, so why do it on vacation? Many resorts and hotels have children's programs or provide babysitters. And the family can split up occasionally, with one parent going off alone or spending time with just one kid.
- Go where you're wanted. Some hotels and restaurants just don't encourage families, so avoid them. Make sure the place you're going to stay will welcome you with your children, has lots of kids staying there and can handle their special needs.
- Each day should have something for everyone. Parents who get bored with theme parks will find museum visits can be fun for children, as long as they don't drag on too long. Kids have lots of energy and need a chance to run around whenever possible. Stop at a playground or park on the way to something else and let them discharge some steam.
- Be realistic about what you can accomplish on a family vacation. You probably won't see and do everything you would like to, and some attractions will have to wait for the next visit. Don't rush around like you do at home. This is a vacation, so adopt a leisurely pace.

  Be flexible and quick to change your plans if things go wrong. "Anxiety is infectious," say Ms. Jordon and Cohen. "If you lose control, the kids probably will too."

Should you use a travel agent? Definitely, if you have a good one. Travel agents don't cost you anything—they are paid commissions by airlines, hotels, car rental companies and tour operators—and can save you money.

If you are a member of the Canadian Automobile Association, you can take advantage of their travel services as well as calling for help if you're stuck on the road. The CAA provides individual Triptik guides: you tell them where you want to go and you get a scenic route mapped out for you.

Each province and state has a tourist office that publishes informative booklets on places to stay and things to do, such as farm vacations, campgrounds and national parks. Get the kids to write for information and put their own names on the return address, so the mail will come to them. Let them point to or circle what they want to do.

Travel and Health Insurance

Don't forget trip cancellation insurance. This is worthwhile, since kids—and adults—get sick suddenly and travel plans must be put on hold. And if you're travelling outside Canada, supplementary medical insurance is a necessity. Most provinces have slashed the amount they pay for health care beyond their own borders, so if you have an accident or get sick while out of the country, the bills can be horrendous. In the United States, a hospital stay can cost as much as $2,000 a day—much more than provincial health plans will cover.

Your employer-sponsored group health insurance plan may pay for out-of-country expenses, or you may have insurance through a bank or trust company's gold credit card or American Express. And you can buy insurance for specific trips from Blue Cross, travel agents, auto and travel clubs and some insurance brokers. (The Canadian Life and Health Insurance Association, 1-800-268-8099, provides a free brochure on travel health insurance and a list of members that offer it.)

Your plan should pay most or all of your costs directly. Don't go for one that makes you pay the bills yourself and apply for reimbursement later. There should also be a toll-free "hot line" number that you can call for assistance at any hour, especially in countries where you don't speak the language.

Also, check whether the plan has no maximum limit or a high limit, say $1 million. Is there a deductible that you pay before the plan kicks in? Does it exclude pre-existing medical conditions and certain dangerous sports, such as scuba diving or para-sailing? Does it pay for your return home in an emergency? Is there a time limit on the coverage and can it be renewed or extended?

If you are planning a trip abroad, consider joining IAMAT, the International Association for Medical Assistance to Travellers. The organization promotes the standardization and coordination of medical care around the world. There are IAMAT doctors in 125 countries who agree to a set payment schedule for members.

Membership is free, though contributions are encouraged. Members get world immunization charts and qualified medical assistance from an English-speaking physician 24 hours a day. You can reach IAMAT at 1287 St. Clair Ave. West, Toronto, Ont. M6E 1B8, telephone (416) 652-0137; and at 40 Regal Rd., Guelph, Ont. N1K 1B5, telephone (519) 836-0102.

By Car, by Plane, by Train

International travel is wonderful, but car trips are still the cheapest and easiest way to go for most families. If you are spending time in the car with kids, here are some tips on making the experience more enjoyable:

- As soon as toddlers can talk, their favourite question is "Are we there yet?" Talk to kids about the distance you're driving and the time it will take to get there. Use terms they can understand. A three-hour car stint, for example, will last as long as a morning at school. Show them the map and let them mark with a crayon how far you've gone.

- Pack plenty of snacks and activities for the car. Audio tapes, whether prerecorded music or stories or your own creations, are a great source of entertainment (and you can borrow them from public libraries). Take crayons or markers, paper, a deck of cards and activity books, and arrange the car so kids can get at things they want without having to undo their seatbelts.
- Expect a car trip with kids to take one-third longer than without, say Jordon and Cohen. Make a pit-stop schedule and stick to it. When you take breaks, try to give the kids some exercise at the same time.
- If a child gets motion sickness, move him or her to the front seat. Restrict reading or writing in the car. Open a window or the air vents. For recurring car sickness, give kids non-prescription Dramamine or Gravol (safe for children as young as two). These drugs are also sedatives and help put kids to sleep.
- If you're renting a car, find out if children's car seats are available and how much they cost. If you need one, reserve it in advance. The rental company will try to sell you several types of insurance, but check to see if your own car insurance policy covers the same areas. Some gold credit cards provide a collision damage waiver on rented vehicles, a good reason to get one of these cards, since rental companies charge $10 to $15 a day for the same coverage.

If you are taking an airplane trip with kids, you can't take as many toys or spread out as much as in the car. Explain to youngsters that their ears will probably hurt when the plane takes off and lands. Keep a handy supply of gum and candies to ease the earaches.

Try to reserve your seat as early as possible. Everyone has a theory about which are the best seats. I like the bulkhead, the one with all the leg room, but Jordon and Cohen point out that the armrests don't move up, so younger kids can't lie comfortably on your lap to rest. They prefer aisle seats. Though kids ask for window seats, the fascination wears off shortly after the plane hits the clouds. As well, they have to disturb others whenever they get out. If the plane has three seats across, book the aisle and the window. Unless the flight is packed, the middle seat will remain empty and you can use it.

Many airlines allow the use of an approved car seat on flights, but some have an upper age limit and others make you pay for the seat, even for kids under two. Ask the airline what its policy is. Ask, too, if there are kids' meals, toy or game packages, disposable diapers and bibs, changing tables in the bathrooms, bottle warming, bassinets, cockpit visits with the flight crew and airport facilities for kids.

Train travel can be fun for kids, as long as the distance is not too long. In a train, you get room to spread out and walk around, food served right at your seat, or in a dining car, accessible bathrooms, lots of scenery outside the windows and a gentle rocking motion that puts babies to sleep for hours.

Accommodation

When you are planning in advance for a place to stay at your destination, look for a hotel or resort that likes children and makes an effort to keep them happy. The hotel you want may not be one that wants your kid. "You can assume that anyplace where the lobby flowers cost more than the rooms will probably not have clowns and free videos," says *Working Woman* magazine in an April 1994 article about taking children along on business trips.

The major chains, such as Holiday Inn and Howard Johnson, often provide special facilities or discounts for kids. Some Delta Hotels offer a supervised child care centre where guests can drop off their children for a few hours for a nominal fee.

All-suite hotels, available in many cities, are ideal for families. They offer more space and cooking facilities yet cost the same as a standard hotel room. You get a separate living room with a sofa bed, a fully equipped kitchen and often two television sets (a real bonus, especially if the kids have brought a video game to hook up).

Before booking a hotel, check to see if it has an indoor or outdoor swimming pool, a refrigerator in the room and special kids' meals at the restaurant. Is there a kids' activity program and how much does it cost? Does the hotel have a family rate or special weekend packages?

A bed and breakfast home is an alternative to a budget hotel or motel. The cost is about the same ($50 to $75 a night) and the food is often better, but you have to do your research. Some homes welcome families, while others frown on kids horsing around in their non-childproofed living rooms. Check with the hosts to see if they have kids of their own and play equipment to share.

Because of the growing popularity of bed and breakfast homes, there are now reservation networks that match up hosts and guests. You don't usually pay a fee, because the agencies work on a commission from the property owners. You can also find many books that describe interesting bed and breakfast homes in various parts of country.

One note of caution: "breakfast" is defined differently at different places. Some provide a continental breakfast, basically toast, rolls or muffins—just enough to tide you over till lunch. Others provide a hearty breakfast of eggs, bacon or sausages, pancakes or French toast. They stuff you so full that you can get through to dinner or at least the late afternoon. Ask specifically about breakfast before you book.

If you are heading to a waterfront or ski resort, you can get more room and a homelike atmosphere by staying in a condominium, apartment or villa. Some are large enough to share with another family. With a full kitchen and dining area, you can cook most of your meals at home and save big bucks on restaurants. Find out about places to rent through travel agents and in newspaper ads.

Cottage rentals are also widely advertised, and there are specialized agencies that handle them. Our family has rented a cottage for the past few summers and found the best setup is one where there are lots of kids nearby and a central meeting place—a public beach, restaurant, game room or activity centre.

When you rent a cottage or vacation home, make sure you ask for detailed information about how the house works and a list of emergency numbers if something breaks down. At one cottage we rented, the pump that drew lake water into the faucets suddenly stopped working. The local plumber's number was posted next to the telephone and he arrived in less than half an hour.

Camping

Camping is not to everyone's taste, but it's one of the most economical vacations you can take. Your kids will enjoy some beautiful scenery while learning about the rhythms of nature. Sitting around the campfire at night, away from the distractions of television, telephones and clocks, children and parents can really talk to each other. Make sure to book well ahead, because campgrounds fill up quickly.

Package Holidays

At the other end of the scale is the all-inclusive package holiday. Club Med, a worldwide network of resorts, has turned its focus from singles to young families, and many cruise ships are wooing families with special kids' and teens' programs. Prices are high, starting at $1,500 to $2,000 a week per person, but that covers airfare, room and board, sports, entertainment and food galore—six or seven meals and snacks a day. And there's the convenience of paying up front and never touching your wallet again. In a tight, self-contained environment, you get time to yourself and your kids make new friends, an important part of a successful vacation.

Theme Parks

If your kids watch TV—and most do, at least on Saturday mornings—they will beg you to take them to theme parks they have seen in commercials. Most parents find these attractions expensive and exhausting but eventually end up going because they can't resist their kids' appeals. To get the most out of your theme park experience, plan ahead. Send for brochures and find out as much as you can about the park to be sure it is appropriate to the ages and interests of your kids. Arrive at the park early when the lines are shorter, and outline your route on a map to save unnecessary walking. Find out where the bathrooms are before you actually need them.

A good safety rule is to teach your kids to call you by your first names. So many kids will be screaming "Mommy" and "Daddy" that you may not be able to distinguish your own child's calls. And make sure you eat properly. If you find it hard to survive on junk food for eight hours, pack a lunch and have a picnic (if the park allows).

As for saving money, there's not much you can do—other than lugging your own food, staying from dawn till dusk and buying a pass for several days in advance, instead of one day at a time. "Theme park vacations are costly," say Ms. Jordon and Cohen. "To go to a park and have to say 'no' to the kids all the time is not fun. So, try to budget generously."

If you need help in planning family vacations, check the resources in the public library and the travel section of your local bookstore. Some cities now have specialty bookstores for travellers. Also, there are many books and magazines giving advice on travelling with babies and kids. An excellent newsletter is *Family Travel Times,* published monthly by Travel With Your Children, 80 Eighth Ave., New York, N.Y. 10011, telephone (212) 206-0688.

Saving Money on Daily Expenses

As parents, we all have developed our own ways of cutting the cost of living. Some tips you pick up from other parents, others you work out yourself. Here are a few of the things I do.

- I save on food by buying in bulk. In our unfinished basement, we store cases of toilet paper, garbage bags, bottled water and non-perishable foods. And we make monthly trips to Price Club, a no-frills warehouse that sells large sizes at big discounts. Laundry detergents, for example, come in 10-litre boxes, much bigger than supermarket packages.
- I keep clothing costs down by dressing my kids in low-priced fleece sweatshirts and sweatpants, which I buy from a discount store. I recycle clothes from one child to the other and resist their pleas for more expensive brand names. They pay the difference themselves if they want something better.
- I cut my kids' hair, a skill I have developed over the years. Richard, now eight, has never been to a barber. Even teenaged Charles still likes my haircuts, though he occasionally goes to a professional. The boys enjoy the convenience of getting their hair trimmed at home, since they watch TV or play video games while I snip. And I love the money I save.
- The walls of the kids' rooms are covered with posters, which they update from time to time as their tastes change. Posters are far cheaper than new paint or wallpaper and provide constant variety.
- When Charles started piano lessons, we rented a secondhand piano for six months to see if he would like it. He did, so we bought it, and the store applied the rental payments to the purchase price.

- I buy packages of blank greeting cards from UNICEF and get the kids to write and illustrate birthday messages to friends and relatives. The cards are not slick, but they are more personal and creative than store-bought cards.

There's nothing unusual here. You probably have tricks just like these to beat the high cost of living. The key is to economize in some areas of daily life so you can splurge in others that really matter to you.

Scrimping and saving all the time is no fun, and like constant dieting, it forces you to break out and binge. So do what you can and don't worry about things you can't do. For example, if you hit the grocery store on your way home from work and you don't bother to use cents-off coupons, forget the guilt. Feel proud of the money you save by buying lower-priced store brands or by cooking tougher meats to perfection.

Even if you cheat a little, your kids will pick up your economical mindset and your cost-saving measures. As long as you're generally strict on keeping to a budget, the odd self-indulgence won't matter.

6 SAVING FOR YOUR CHILD'S EDUCATION

Almost from the moment our children arrive, we start thinking and worrying about the cost of post-secondary education. Although tuition fees are lower in Canada than in the United States, they're climbing rapidly, and at a much faster rate than the cost of living. Tuition for undergraduate arts students went up 58 per cent in the five years ending in spring 1993, while the cost of living rose just 16 per cent over the same period.

Since tuition accounts for only 15 to 20 per cent of universities' income, and provincial governments are squeezed for money, fee increases are inevitable. Throw in room and board, books, transportation and personal expenses, and the annual cost of sending a child to university can be staggering—especially if you have several studying at the same time. For most parents, it's too much to finance from current income. So we have to save in advance.

If you are sending a child to university, college or trade school this year, you can expect an annual bill of $8,000 to $10,000 if the student lives away from home. But if costs continue rising at a 7-per-cent annual clip, as they have in the past, college bills for today's preschooler will total about $90,000 by the time he or she finishes a four-year degree.

Of course, you may want your children to pay their own way, and that's a valid option. As parents, we're happy to see our kids take responsibility for their education. But there's a limit to how much students can earn from part-time and summer jobs, especially when the economy is slow and even university graduates find it hard to get work.

Financing Before Your Child Goes to School

In today's competitive society, a post-secondary degree is still the ticket to better jobs and career prospects for young people. So we parents have to motivate our kids to stay in school. One way to do it is to put aside money for their education from the early years and keep reminding them that the money is there.

How much you save is less important than how early you get into the habit of putting money away. Even $25 to $50 a month can make a difference if you do it regularly from the time your children are toddlers. If they get jobs and earn money for college later, all the better. They can pay for extras and you can pay for essentials.

Here are some ways to save for a child's education over a period of 10 to 20 years.

Buy a Registered Education Savings Plan

Established in 1960 by the federal government, RESPs are a tax shelter intended to help families save for post-secondary education. Over the years, the number of plans has sprouted and they have become more flexible. Parents can contribute to them and grandparents too, but they are not restricted to family members. You can buy a registered education savings plan for a friend's child, godchild, stepchild or the child of your same-sex partner.

But there's one feature common to all plans—you can't count on getting any return on your investment. And that's a big gamble. Think of an RESP as a lottery. If your child goes to college or university, you win. If he or she finishes only high school or drops out after starting a post-secondary program, you lose. All you get back is the money you paid in over the years. The earnings on that money pay for the education of someone else's child.

Despite the risk, RESPs appeal to many parents. I started a plan for my son Charles, partly because there wasn't much else around in 1981 when he was born. Finding myself tempted to spend the monthly baby bonus rather than save it, I put it in an RESP and liked how the money was locked in and couldn't be tapped for other purposes. The baby bonus is no longer universal, and many parents, myself included, no longer receive it. But I still keep up my monthly RESP payments.

When Richard was born in 1986, my father bought an RESP with a single lump-sum contribution. Our sons know we have put away money for their education and we hope that's an incentive to keep them going. RESP sponsors give you a certificate with your child's name on it, suggesting you frame it and post it in a prominent place in your house. This provides a daily reminder to children that their college education is (at least partially) prepaid.

You can start an education savings plan when your baby arrives. Most parents do it before the age of two, and that makes sense, since payments are lower the earlier you start. Or you can wait till you have a sense of how well your child is doing at school. But it's not as important any more for your child to be a gifted student because RESPs will cover non-academic courses too.

Affluent grandparents can no longer make a one-time deposit that covers the full cost of a child's RESP. The tax rules changed in 1990, and now the money has to be doled out in amounts of no more than $1,500 a year—or you will be subject to a penalty tax of 1 per cent a month on overpayments. You and your spouse can each have a plan for the same beneficiary, but the total amount contributed must not exceed $1,500 a year.

You can contribute to an RESP for 21 years from the opening date and the plan can remain open for 26 years. The maximum you can put into the plan is $31,500. You can't deduct RESP contributions from your income (unlike a registered retirement savings plan, for which contributions are tax-deductible). But RESP earnings will grow tax-free until the plan is collapsed.

This tax sheltering can make a big difference to your investment returns. If you invest the maximum $125 a month over 15 years in an RESP earning 12 per cent a year, your investment will grow to $62,448. The same amount invested without the benefit of RESP and earning the same 12 per cent a year will grow to only $38,271 after taxes, assuming a marginal tax rate of 45 per cent. The income earned within the RESP is more than $24,000 ahead.

When the RESP matures, the principal is returned tax-free. That's because it came from after-tax dollars and never earned a tax deduction. The income paid to the child is taxed in his or her hands. Since students generally have low earnings and special tax credits available to them, they are likely to be in a lower tax bracket than their parents. Often, they pay little or no tax on the money.

There are several kinds of RESPs. The oldest and probably best known—you see their brochures just about everywhere—are the pooled plans offered by Canadian Scholarship Trust, University Scholarships of Canada, Heritage Scholarship Trust, Universitas Foundation of Canada and Children's Education Trust of Canada. Together, they have more than $1 billion invested in them.

With a pooled RESP, you make regular fixed payments over a period of years. There is little or no flexibility to vary the payments, though you're given a grace period if you fall behind. You can also buy optional insurance to continue payments if you die or become totally disabled.

When your child starts a post-secondary program, he or she gets a refund of the money paid into the plan (minus administration fees) in the first year, then qualifies for assistance payments for up to three more years. Since interest rates vary and so does the dropout rate, the exact payments cannot be predicted in advance. There is no guarantee they will pay for the complete costs of an education.

Because you're already taking a gamble with a pooled RESP, you don't have to worry about risky investments. Your money goes into conservative interest vehicles, not stocks. Over the past five years, the plans have shown an average return of 10 to 12 per cent a year. They earn higher interest rates than an individual would because of the size of their investments.

Successful students get even more than the stated rate of return because of the dropout or attrition factor. This is hard to predict because it changes each year. University Scholarships of Canada asked an actuary to calculate the effective return on investment for students whose plans matured in 1989 and who qualified for assistance payments in 1990, 1991 and 1992. It ranged from 14.3 to 16.1 per cent.

Pooled RESPs are what's known as a zero sum game. If you win, someone else loses. In the past, about 25 to 30 per cent of beneficiaries failed to reach university or dropped out before graduating, and their contributions went to those who did complete their studies. Today, the eligibility rules have loosened up and the attrition rate has dropped to less than 10 per cent, so contributors get a smaller premium over the prevailing level of interest rates. (For this reason, some parents resist any changes to make the plans even more flexible.)

The plans have been criticized for high up-front marketing costs. You buy one or more RESP units for each child, depending on how much you want to save. Sponsors charge an enrollment fee, generally $100 to $200 a unit, which is deducted from your payments in the early years. These fees can add up if you buy several units, as most parents do. If you drop out of the plan before maturity, the fees are deducted from your refund. So before making a commitment, make sure it's for an amount you can live with if your income varies.

There is some legal protection for buyers, since RESPs are regulated by provincial securities commissions. Sponsors have to file a prospectus, a document outlining all terms, conditions and costs. Read the prospectus carefully before making any decisions.

Overzealous sales can be a problem. Pooled plans, though marketed by non-profit foundations, are tied closely to profit-making distributors. They are sold through commissioned salespeople who offer kickbacks for referrals and compete fiercely for business. This results in occasional high-pressure sales tactics more typical of driveway-paving and aluminum-siding contractors.

Watch out for sales reps who claim that RESPs are covered by the Canada Deposit Insurance Corp. They're not, though some of their investments may be government-guaranteed. Take time to compare plans and don't get spooked by spurious deadlines to sign a contract. Some provinces give you a 60-day cooling-off period, so you can back out if you change your mind.

Recently, individual RESPs have been introduced by mutual fund companies, brokerage firms, banks and trust companies. With these plans, you make your own investment choices. But you are also responsible for monitoring results and changing strategies when required.

Most self-directed plans use mutual funds as the investment vehicle. You are advised to start with more volatile growth funds, then switch to safer fixed-income funds as your child gets closer to college. You get a wide range of funds to choose from, either from the same company (if your plan is with a mutual fund firm or bank) or from various companies (if your plan is with a brokerage firm).

Self-directed RESPs offer tremendous flexibility. You can name several beneficiaries and remove or add them at any time. Even you, the subscriber, can be an eligible beneficiary. It's fun to imagine giving up the daily grind of earning a living and going back to school full-time, with most costs already covered.

A self-directed plan is also more convenient. You can start and stop payments whenever you please, interrupting your contributions for a while if you have other priorities. When your child heads off to college, you don't receive a fixed amount every year, as with a pooled plan. You and your child can agree on a schedule of withdrawals that suits your needs. Another bonus is that you can remove the original capital at any time before maturity—without penalty—if an unexpected financial need crops up. The interest income will remain and grow tax-free inside the plan.

But remember that the flexibility only goes so far. If there are no family members ready and willing to further their studies on a full-time basis, the RESP income must be paid to a school you designate when you set up the plan. And since the money was sheltered from tax, you do not get a tax credit for your donation. You forfeit all the income built up over the years, which may equal or exceed your original contributions.

Here are some questions to ask about RESPs when meeting with a sales representative and comparing plans:

- How much do I pay to set up a pooled plan and keep it going? The enrollment fees are deducted from payments in the early years and not refunded. But one plan, Heritage Scholarship Trust, gives back enrollment fees at maturity. You may also face annual depository fees (about $7.50 to $10) and annual administration fees (about 0.5 per cent of the total fund).
- If I buy mutual fund units, what are the costs? Funds sold through a commissioned sales force usually have

either an up-front fee (deducted from the initial contributions) or a deferred sales charge (deducted from the redemption proceeds, often on a higher value). Find out if there are fees to switch from one mutual fund to another. How much is the management-expense ratio, the amount deducted from the fund's assets each year to pay for portfolio advisory services and other costs? Depending on the type of fund, the management-expense ratio ranges from 1 to 2.5 per cent a year. Is there an account setup fee, an annual trustee fee or a charge for withdrawals and change of beneficiaries?

- What are the eligibility requirements? Find out what educational institutions qualify for the plan. Most cover colleges and universities outside Canada, but some have restrictions on non-academic programs. Would a two-year community college course qualify, or a one-year trade school course? What happens if the child takes a one-year break after finishing high school or drops out of a post-secondary program and returns later? Some pooled plans will not pay if the child interrupts his or her studies. Does the payout depend on the child's passing the previous year? What if he or she takes summer make-up courses?
- How much will my child receive in the second, third and possibly fourth year of studies? If the salesperson gives you projections, what future interest rates are those projections based on? Are the projections "industry averages" or actual experiences with the plan you are considering? Some plans are new and have no track record.
- What if my child does not go to university or college? Most plans will let you transfer the funds to another family member, but the pooled plans prohibit changes beyond the age of 13 or 14. They make an exception

for children with severe mental or physical problems that prevent them from undertaking post-secondary studies. A self-directed plan generally allows you to make changes at any time, right up to university.

- Can I sell my RESP? If your child is not college-bound and no one else in the family is interested, it makes sense to sell the plan to someone who can use it. But if you do find a buyer, a sale price may be difficult to establish, and there are tax implications to keep in mind. The buyer will have to factor in any tax the student pays on the money as it is withdrawn. And you, the seller, will have to pay tax on the sale proceeds. Revenue Canada has ruled that being paid to name another person's child as an RESP beneficiary constitutes a taxable capital gain.

Put Money in Your Child's Savings Account

In the days of the universal baby bonus, many parents deposited the monthly government cheque in a savings account earmarked for their child's education. As the money accumulated, they would buy a guaranteed investment certificate or Canada Savings Bond. As long as the payments were invested "in trust" for the child, the income was not taxable in the parent's hands.

In January 1993, Ottawa brought in a more targeted child tax benefit for lower-income families. If you are eligible for this payment, you can still put some or all of it in a savings account in trust for the child without worrying about the tax consequences. Earnings are taxed in the child's hands, which means no tax is payable unless his or her income is more than about $6,500, the basic personal exemption.

Suppose you don't get the child tax benefit. Well, you can still put money in a savings account in trust for the child, but the income will be attributable to you for tax purposes. This will continue until the child turns 18, after which the attribution rules no longer apply. If interest rates remain low, your savings will grow slowly after tax and may fall short of what you need. So don't leave the money in a savings account. Transfer funds to a higher-growth investment as soon as you get enough.

You don't have to set up a formal trust for a child's account. A trust involves up-front legal fees and ongoing administration fees, since you have to file a separate tax return each year. Using a trust really only makes sense if large sums are involved. But it will ensure the money is used for education and not for something frivolous like a European stint or a Harley-Davidson motorbike.

Most institutions will accept your word that the funds are in trust for the child. But to protect the money, keep the child's trust account at a different institution than the one where you do all your banking. If both are in the same place, the bank can legally dip into the child's account to cover a shortfall in your chequing or credit card accounts. You may not be aware that in the fine print on the back of an application to open an account, you authorize the bank to have access to any deposits in your name—even an account opened in trust for a child.

The lack of security for children's trust accounts also becomes a consideration when parents split up. Toronto financial advisor Tom Delaney cites a case of a couple who separated after 25 years of marriage. The husband had opened a trust account with a stockbroker for the children's education and was the only signatory, although relatives and friends had contributed to it. The issue of control over the trust funds was not dealt with during the separation, and the wife discovered her estranged husband had withdrawn large sums for personal needs. Moreover, the broker had the right to dip into the children's account any time the husband's margin account fell below the limit. To prevent this kind of abuse, talk to your financial institution about tighter rules for access to and reimbursement of children's trust funds. If you can't get reassurance, consider setting up a formal trust.

Invest in Mutual Funds or Company Shares

If you want your money to work hard for you over the long term, you need something more than a savings account. For maximum growth, consider putting a portion of the money in stocks or mutual funds. Equity investments offer tax benefits that rival those involved in an RESP—and without all the eligibility restrictions that a registered plan imposes.

When you invest in Canadian stocks or equity funds, you earn dividends, which are taxed at a lower rate than interest. The rationale is that dividends are paid out of company profits that have already been taxed. Once you factor in the dividend tax credit, $1 in dividends is worth about $1.30 in interest on an after-tax basis.

You also earn a capital gain when you sell your stocks or equity funds (assuming, of course, they have gone up in value since you bought them). Capital gains are still attractive from a tax point of view, despite the recent elimination of the $100,000 lifetime capital gains exemption.

Like dividends, capital gains carry a lower tax rate than interest. You include only 75 per cent of a capital gain in your income for tax purposes. If you are in the highest marginal tax bracket, you pay tax at a rate of 35 to 40 per cent on capital gains, compared with 50 per cent or more on interest income.

Another advantage is that capital gains are taxed only when an investment is sold, yielding a considerable tax deferral. Suppose you buy shares of a telephone company at $10 apiece when your child is born. Two decades later, the shares are worth $40 and you finally sell them. The $30-a-share gain builds up tax-free over the years.

Equity funds are a little different from stocks. The fund managers distribute and pay out capital gains each year as investments are sold. However, the profit you make as the fund's unit value goes up is not taxed until you sell.

Investments that produce capital gains are appealing for college savings because the gains are taxable in the child's hands—unlike interest and dividends, which accrue back to the parent. Capital gains stay with the child. So by holding stocks or mutual funds in trust for a child and cashing them in during the college years, you get both a tax deferral and a tax saving. The day of reckoning comes only when the investments are sold and the student is responsible for the tax bill. This is essentially the same tax shelter as an RESP, but without the risk of forfeiting income by not attending a full post-secondary program.

And, best of all, the money is not restricted to higher education. You and your child can agree to use it for private school, summer camp, travel abroad or any other purpose.

There is one key difference. Parents must pay tax on dividends or distributions from their children's equity investments, while dividends build up tax-free in an RESP. But you can minimize taxes by choosing stocks or mutual funds that emphasize capital gains over income. Instead of high-yield telephone company shares, find a small and fast-growing technology stock that pays no dividends. Or instead of a broad-based equity fund, try an emerging markets fund or one that specializes in small stocks.

Isn't this a risky strategy? Yes, it certainly can be, since equity investments go up and down as economic conditions change. The trick is to be patient and take a long-term view. Over a period of 10 years or more, stocks generally come out ahead of other investments—at least, they have in the past over almost any 10-year period you choose. And if you hold a diversified mutual fund, one that holds a broad selection of companies in various industries and countries, you increase your odds of getting a superior return.

Don't try to outguess the market. Just find a solid mutual fund with a consistent long-term track record and add money regularly. When your child hits 11 or 12, start to protect your gains. Put any new money into guaranteed investment certificates that mature as the university term begins. Gradually transfer out of equity funds—say by moving 10 per cent each year—into more stable money market funds, term deposits or GICs.

Your savings will lose purchasing power sitting in more conservative investments. But you don't want to take the risk of running into a stock market crash or prolonged slump at the same time the college bills come due. Don't cash out all your equities. Keep some money in stocks for your child's later years of undergraduate or perhaps post-graduate studies.

Buy Stripped Bonds or Coupons

"Strips" are federal or provincial government bonds with the interest coupons removed. They pay interest not twice a year as other bonds do, but only on the maturity date. You buy them at a deep discount to the face value and hold them for periods of one to 20 years or more. The attraction is that if interest rates rise, you can lock in a high rate for a long time and you know exactly how much you will receive down the road.

Strips are a popular investment for RRSPs, but they're not really suitable for non-registered educational savings. That's because the built-up interest is attributed back to the parent annually for tax purposes, even though it is not paid till maturity. You will be paying tax on money you don't receive. Since 1984, investment dealers selling strip bonds are required to supply buyers with an information sheet that explains this tax wrinkle.

If, however, the grandparents live outside Canada, they can buy stripped bonds for a child's college fund and not have to worry about income attribution. These rules apply only to Canadian residents.

There are other problems with strips, such as high commissions that are built into the price and not disclosed to buyers. You have to find several dealers with the same bond in their inventory and compare prices. And be prepared for extreme volatility. The value of these long-term investments will reflect and magnify any change in interest rates. If rates have gone up since you bought your strip, you may have to take a distress price to sell it before maturity—if you can unload it at all. Try to hang on if you can.

Buy Life Insurance as a Savings Vehicle

Life insurance agents often urge parents to take out a policy on a child's life and pay the premiums. Instead of buying a term life policy that provides only protection, you choose a cash-value policy that has an element of savings. Later, you transfer the life insurance to the child on a tax-free basis when he or she turns 18.

As with an RESP, the child withdraws cash from the insurance policy as needed over the three or four years of a post-secondary program and pays little or no tax. But life insurance is more flexible than an RESP because the funds can be used for a college education or other needs—such as getting married, buying a house, starting a business or just travelling. Moreover, many policies will provide insurance on the contributing parent's life in case he or she dies before the plan matures.

Canada Life, for example, has what it calls a Youth Plan. An agent gave me an illustration, showing that if you take out a $50,000 whole life policy on a newborn, you will pay premiums of $61.50 a month, or $738 a year. Part of the money goes into a savings fund, which will accumulate $16,281 for college costs by the time the child turns 20. But the cash buildup, based on 1994 interest rates, is not guaranteed. Always ask if you can get a worst-case scenario, showing the effect of lower investment returns.

To make life insurance more attractive as a savings vehicle, the industry has developed a new product called universal life. This combines lower-priced term insurance with a tax-deferred investment fund. It is more flexible than whole life insurance, and you can pay for your insurance premiums from a pool of investments sheltered from tax. "If you're in the top marginal tax bracket, this [universal life] can cut the actual cost of insurance in half," say authors James Bullock and George Brett in *Insure Sensibly: A Guide to Life and Disability Insurance.*

The real question is: Does a child really need life insurance? Luckily, few children die before their parents and they usually have no income to replace. The major expense is funeral costs, which can be covered with a small amount of insurance, say $5,000 or $10,000. Life insurance agents argue that a guaranteed death benefit can be helpful if your child later develops a health condition that makes him or her uninsurable. But this is not all that common.

The tax rules for universal life link your contribution to the amount of insurance you buy. So if you don't want to insure a child, you will have to buy more insurance for yourself—assuming you aren't already insured or need to top up your coverage.

For most of us, it's better to separate our insurance and investment needs rather than bundle them together. Mixing the two makes it harder to shop and compare products. Buying life insurance for investment purposes requires the expertise of an advisor familiar with insurance concepts, taxation and investing.

Universal life is particularly complex and can be difficult to evaluate. Ask about the true rate of return on savings after the insurance cost is deducted. If the agent uses long-term projections, find out what assumptions are behind them. Are they based on realistic forecasts for interest rates, inflation and equity markets?

Ask, too, about the insurance part of the contract. Term insurance is cheap in the early years and gets expensive later. Is there a guaranteed maximum premium that cannot be exceeded? Or does the company offer term-to-100 insurance, with level premiums all the way? Find out what are the annual administration and management fees and if they also are guaranteed.

Pay Off the Mortgage More Quickly

When a child is born, a family's income is often stretched to the limit and there is little extra money to put aside for education. Why not devote your energies to getting rid of your biggest debt, the mortgage on the family home? Paying off the mortgage will free up cash flow, which you can use to pay for college later on. Many parents (and financial planners too) prefer this strategy to starting an education fund.

There are many ways to shrink the mortgage. You can make prepayments—most institutions let you pay down 10 per cent of the principal each year—or raise your monthly payments, or go onto a schedule of weekly or biweekly payments. Some lenders give you the option of doubling up your payments occasionally.

To see how these strategies can reduce your mortgage balance and overall interest costs, buy a low-cost financial software program (most are in the $50 range) and run some numbers. Or ask your lender or lawyer for a revised amortization schedule. Even a small adjustment can shave years off the remaining life of the mortgage.

Suppose you have a $100,000 mortgage, amortized over 25 years at a rate of 12 per cent. Your monthly payments are $1,031.90 and you will have handed over $209,569 in interest when the mortgage is paid off in 25 years. You can cut this interest dramatically by switching to weekly payments and adding a small amount to directly pay down the principal. By paying $257.98 a week, you will discharge the mortgage in 17.5 years and reduce the interest to $133,131, a saving of $76,438.

With hard work and good timing, you can get rid of the mortgage and still have a few years to go before your children finish high school. At that time, you and your partner may be earning significantly higher incomes. Once the mortgage payments are out of the way, continue setting aside a similar amount but put it into a college fund. You should not invest as aggressively as a parent who started earlier, since you have only a short time to save, but you can allocate a portion to growth investments.

If you're short of money for the children's education, you can always borrow on the equity in your paid-up house. You do this by taking out a new first mortgage to pay for college expenses, or by using the house as collateral for a line of credit or personal loan. With good security, lenders will give you a break on interest costs.

Invest Your Child's Earnings

If your child has a part-time or summer job, encourage him or her to deposit the money in a separate bank account and invest it for college. The resulting investment income will be taxed in the child's hands and won't be attributable to you. Then, you give the child an equivalent amount for spending money.

Even better, if you have your own business, you can pay your child a salary for work performed. These should be bona fide business services such as stuffing envelopes, delivering flyers or counting money, and the amounts paid should be reasonable. Again, this money can be invested in the child's name at his or her low tax rate.

Set Up a Trust for Educational Purposes

If you or your child's grandparents have a lot of money—$100,000 is usually the minimum needed to justify administrative fees—you can set up a living or "inter vivos" trust and give or lend funds to the trust interest-free. The money may come from investments, an inheritance, the sale of a house or a family business.

Trusts are complex, and expert advice is essential. Both a lawyer and an accountant should be involved in structuring a trust, since there can be enormous tax penalties if you make a mistake. What follows are general guidelines only.

Before 1985, living trusts were popular for income splitting among family members with different tax rates. But hot tax-saving ideas usually don't last, and this one was hit by changes in the income attribution rules. Now when you give or lend money to a trust, all the income earned on the original amount will be taxed in your hands—except if the children are over 18. This takes away much of the tax-saving benefits.

However, the reinvested income will not come back to you. Say you lend $100,000 to a trust and it earns 8 per cent annually. The entire first year's income of $8,000 is attributed to you. But in the second year, the $640 earned on the first year's income can be allocated to the children. Over time, the "second generation" income is substantial and will grow to more than the income earned on the original loan.

Also, as we saw before, capital gains escape the attribution rules. So you can achieve some income-splitting by investing the trust assets for capital growth rather than dividends and interest income. The gains will be taxed in your children's hands. But don't take too many risks. If you are the trustee, you are responsible for investing the money prudently on your children's behalf.

As trustee, you control both the capital and the distribution of income. Trust income is taxed at the highest marginal tax rate, but you can save taxes by making what is known as a preferred beneficiary election. This means the trust's income is allocated to the children and taxed in their hands but not actually paid out to them. The trust's accumulated income can be used for the children's education or any other need you think worthwhile. When the trust has served its purpose, it can be wound up and any loans repaid. So you can get back your original capital.

A living trust may be suitable for grandparents who are planning to leave large gifts to charity in their wills. A charitable bequest doesn't provide any tax relief to them during their lifetimes, only to their estate. They can achieve the same purpose and get a tax break with what is known as a charitable remainder trust.

Essentially, the grandparents contribute cash or other property to the trust and name the charity as beneficiary of the capital after they die. In return, they get an immediate tax credit, based on the amount involved and their age and life expectancy. The charity can be an educational institution, such as a Canadian or U.S. university. The income earned by the trust is used for educational purposes, and after one or both grandparents die, the capital goes to the charity. An added benefit is that the assets in the trust do not become part of their estate, thus avoiding probate fees.

A warning is in order here. The federal government is currently reviewing the rules for taxation of trusts, in response to critics who say there is room for abuse. Talk to a professional advisor about the implications of this review on your tax and estate planning activities.

Buy a One-Year Investment for a Child of 17

The attribution rules, as we saw before, force parents to pay tax on income generated by their gifts to a child. But these rules no longer apply once your son or daughter turns 18. So why not buy a one-year guaranteed investment certificate for a 17-year-old child? When it matures, the child will be taxed on the income. You face no tax liability.

This is a way to get money into your child's hands basically tax-free as he or she heads off to university. But it depends on your willingness to entrust a large amount to a child without any formal restrictions on how it is used. A trust may be required if you want to keep the money from being blown on non-essentials.

Financing While Your Child Is at School

Student Loans, Grant and Awards

Flash forward 18 years. Your baby has graduated from high school with good enough marks to be accepted at the post-secondary program of his or her choice. The moment of truth has arrived. Is there enough in the kitty to cover all the costs?

If there is, congratulations. If not, you and your child can apply for grants, scholarships and student loans to fill the gap. There are a number of government and private programs, each with differing conditions for eligibility.

- The federal government's Canada Student Loans Program is available to students who can show need, based on their parents' income. (Exceptions are made in cases where a student is considered independent of his or her parents.) The program is administered by each of the provinces except Quebec, which has its own student loans program.

As long as the student maintains a 60 per cent average in full-time degree studies, he or she does not have to repay the loan until six months after graduating. The interest rate is set each year by the federal government, and payments can be stretched over a period of up to nine and a half years.

In the past, many student loans were never repaid, so Ottawa has handed over the job of collection to the chartered banks, which are more serious about cracking down on delinquent loans. One idea they are talking about is reporting debtors' names to credit bureaus. This puts the onus on students to make prompt repayments or lose their good credit rating.

A full description of the student loan program is available from the Department of the Secretary of State, Canada Student Loans Program, Student Assistance Directorate, P.O. Box 2090, Station D, Ottawa, Ont. K1P 6C6.

A booklet worth getting is "Hot 100: A Guide to What the Feds Are Doing for Youth," which lists work, study and travel programs funded by the federal government. Write to the Communications Department, Ministry of Human Resources Development, Hull, Que. K1A 0J9.

- In addition to administering the Canada Student Loans Program, provincial governments provide aid for students who can show they lack financial means. They may be eligible for loans and bursaries in the province where they live or the province where they plan to study.

Here are addresses of provincial aid offices:

Newfoundland: Student Aid Division, Department of Education, Thomson Student Centre, Memorial University, St. John's, Nfld. A1C 5S7.

Prince Edward Island: Student Aid Division, Department of Education, Box 2000, Charlottetown, P.E.I. C1A 7N8.

Nova Scotia: Student Assistance Division, Department of Advanced Education and Job Training, P.O. Box 2290, Station M, Halifax, N.S. B3J 3C8.

New Brunswick: Student Financial Support Services, Department of Advanced Education and Training, Centennial Building, P.O. Box 6000, Fredericton, N.B. E3B 5H1.

Quebec: Students Financial Aid, Department of Education, Quebec City, Que. G1R 5K9.

Ontario: Student Awards Branch, Ministry of Education and Training, Keskus Mall, P.O. Box 4500, Station P, Thunder Bay, Ont. P7B 6G9.

Manitoba: Student Aid Branch, Department of Education, P.O. Box 6, 693 Taylor Ave., Winnipeg, Man. R3M 2T9.

Saskatchewan: Student Financial Assistance, Saskatchewan Education, 1855 Victoria Ave., Regina, Sask. S4P 3V5.

Alberta: Students Finance Board, Department of Advanced Education, 10th floor, Baker Centre, 10025–106th St., Edmonton, Alta. T5J 1G4.

British Columbia: Student Services Branch, Department of Advanced Education and Job Training, Parliament Buildings, 818 Broughton St., Victoria, B.C. V8V 1X4.

Yukon: Advanced Education Branch, Department of Education, Box 2703, Whitehorse, Y. T. Y1A 2C6.

Northwest Territories: Student Services, Department of Education, Yellowknife, N.W.T. X0E 2L9.

- There are a number of scholarships, grants and bursaries from private sources such as foundations and corporations. They are usually available to students who show high levels of academic achievement and do not have to be repaid. Some are awarded automatically, but most require an application through university and provincial financial aid offices. Usually the student applies, not the parents. The Association of Universities and Colleges of Canada administers a number of private scholarship programs. For a list, contact the AUCC's Awards Division, 600–350 Albert St., Ottawa, Ont. K1R 1B1.

- Banks offer loans and lines of credit to students who do not qualify for government assistance. The loans, once based on the parents' ability to pay, are now often targeted to students and may not need a cosigner. Banks use the opportunity to sell students other services, such as banking packages, credit cards and registered retirement savings plans.

The maximum loan is about $5,000 a year, or up to $25,000 or $30,000 for a four-year undergraduate program. But unlike government loans, which don't have to be repaid till after graduation, bank loans must be repaid while the child is still in school. Students pay the monthly interest while in school and begin repaying the principal six months to a year after graduation.

- Some universities run all year round and provide work-study programs which combine academic courses with relevant—and salaried—work experience. Co-op programs exist in almost all disciplines at 45 universities and 96 colleges and institutes in Canada.

Housing Options for Students

Suppose your child goes away to school but doesn't want to live in a dormitory. You can save on residence costs and get a tax break too by buying a house or condo apartment near the university for the use of your child and a few fellow students. You as owner can hire your child as property manager and pay him or her a salary to take care of the property and collect rents.

Spending $30,000 to $40,000 as a downpayment on a house or apartment near campus will ensure your child has a reasonable place to live and at a good rent. The fellow students may be well known to your son or daughter, so there's a certain safety for you as landlord.

There are tax benefits involved in owning rental property. You can write off mortgage interest as an expense, as well as property taxes, insurance, utilities, repairs and maintenance. You can also claim depreciation or capital cost allowance on the property but you don't have to. All these expenses will reduce or eliminate the tax payable on your rental income and may give you a loss you can claim against other income.

When you sell the house in the future, you will have to recapture the capital cost allowance you've already claimed in your income. The tax is postponed, not eliminated. But a tax deferral can be a saving, as long as you're aware of the bill to pay later on.

There are tax benefits for your child too. He or she is earning a salary as property manager and is entitled to claim personal tax credits and deductions on the income. Meanwhile, you can write off that salary as a business expense.

Kevyn Nightingale, a Toronto chartered accountant, suggests that parents arrange to have the child share in the growth in value of the rental property. If the property sells for a higher price when eventually sold, the gain can be taxed in the child's hands. But he advises caution, since the business of transferring a capital gain is tricky and not for do-it-yourselfers. "It's too complicated, too easy to mess up, and too many things can go wrong. A professional will see that it's done properly."

Of course, the property may not gain in value and you may not get the price you paid, so you must be prepared to hold on for longer than three or four years. There are other risks too. You may have to do major repairs or renovations to make the house suitable for students, plus invest in big cleanups when the school year ends.

Also, your freshman student may be too busy with school or social activities to be a reliable property manager. It depends on his or her maturity, which only you can assess. Has he or she been responsible for cleanups and maintenance in your home (and not just their own room)? Can he or she deal with emergencies or will you get panic calls at night and have to make long-distance arrangements?

Tax Credits and Deductions for Students

Don't forget about annual tax returns for students. The April 30 tax deadline comes at a bad time, right in the middle of final exams, and is easy to ignore if no tax is owing. However, valuable tax credits can be missed if a return is not filed. So parents should do it on behalf of their children, if necessary.

If the student's 1994 employment income is less than $6,456 (after deductions), he or she will probably not have to pay tax but will qualify for tax credits and deductions:

- The goods and services tax credit is paid quarterly to those who file annual returns.
- There is a tuition fee credit equal to 17 per cent of the fees paid. (If tuition is $2,000, this is worth $340.) In addition, there is an education credit of $80 a month for each month spent as a full-time student. A tax credit

reduces the tax payable on earned income. If the child has a low income and cannot use the credit, a supporting parent or grandparent can claim it, up to a maximum of $680. (It can also be claimed by the student's spouse, if there is one.) You must attach an official tax receipt from the university (form T2202A) to the tax return to qualify for the credit.

- On a Quebec a tax return, a student may deduct tuition fees of more than $100. There is no tax credit, nor is the deduction transferable. Parents in Quebec can claim their children as dependents when they are full-time students in post-secondary institutions.
- Moving expenses are deductible when the child moves 40 kilometres or more to a new place of residence. When moving to school, students can deduct expenses only against taxable scholarship or grant money. (The first $500 of this income is tax-free.) But they can also claim moving expenses when moving away from school to take a job, even if the move is back home for the summer. The expenses can be deducted against their summer employment income.

Since students are unlikely to keep track of their expenses, it's up to you to urge them to do so. The incentive is lower taxes for the student and possibly the parent too. For example, moving expenses reduce the child's net income, which means the supporting parent may be able to claim him or her as a dependent.

Single parents should also keep in mind the equivalent-to-spouse exemption. If you are divorced and supporting a child under 18, you may be able to claim the student at the spousal rate—and this can be very rewarding.

RRSPs

If your children are earning money from part-time jobs, encourage them to open a registered retirement savings plan.

Starting an RRSP at a young age means the earnings can grow tax-free for many years. Get them into the habit of putting 10 cents of each dollar they earn into the plan.

Never mention the word "retirement" to a teenager. It's a real turnoff. A better way to explain an RRSP is as a money machine—a way to turn a hundred dollars into a million dollars through long-term compound growth in a tax-sheltered environment. Show the child how much his or her money will grow if deposited in an early-bird RRSP and left there for decades. There is also a tax deduction, but many students can't use it since their incomes are too low.

If all their earnings are needed for immediate spending, or even if they earn nothing at all, your children can still have an RRSP if you put money in for them. This is a strategy that works only for adult children, those 19 or older.

Under the tax rules, Canadians can make a lifetime overcontribution to an RRSP of up to $8,000 beyond their specified limit. Parents or grandparents with some surplus cash can contribute to an RRSP for adult children—whether the children have earned income or not—to get them started. Later, as the children earn more, they can get a tax break by deducting these RRSP contributions—and keep the money in their pockets.

If your adult children are working and have RRSP-eligible income, then you can simply put money into a plan for them. This would count as a regular contribution, not an overcontribution. To ensure the kids do not cash in the RRSPs when the going gets tough, you can invest it in five-year GICs. Keep rolling them over when they mature.

Financial planner Marie Howes of Mississauga, Ontario, has an example of how helpful these contributions can be. Take two students, Susan and Thomas, who have finished university and started their first jobs. They are each earning $26,000 a year, not a great amount, and they have student loans to pay off, apartments to equip and working clothes to buy.

Susan's parents, aware of her inability to save for retirement, decide to help her get ahead by contributing $2,000 annually to an RRSP for her over nine years. They invest in five-year GICs earning 7.5 per cent. Susan never makes another RRSP contribution after her parents' nine-year commitment is over.

Thomas's parents prefer that he inherit anything that is left when they die. When Thomas is finally able to contribute to an RRSP, he is 32 years old. After that, he diligently contributes $2,000 a year to age 65.

When Susan and Tom are both 65, their RRSPs are worth roughly the same amount. Susan's RRSP has grown to $255,767, even though her parents originally contributed only $18,000. Thomas has contributed $68,000 over the years and his RRSP has grown to $256,517. It has taken him more than 30 years to catch up to Susan. This is an example of the time value of money and the power of compounding.

Making RRSP contributions for our children is an excellent way to teach them the importance of early financial planning.

7 TEACHING YOUR CHILDREN ABOUT MONEY

In many homes, children know as little about family finances as they do about their parents' sexual practices. That's certainly how it was when I grew up. I knew my family was well off because we had a nice house in a nice neighbourhood. But my father kept all of us in the dark about money, including my mother.

Today's parents share more with their children, but there are still homes where a serious discussion of money is taboo when youngsters are listening. We want to preserve our children's innocence and avoid burdening them with financial problems they are too young to understand. And sometimes, we shut them out for a more selfish reason—to prevent them from broadcasting confidential personal information to friends, teachers, neighbours or anyone who shows an interest.

But ignorance is not always bliss. While it's unnecessary—and probably undesirable—for parents to share every financial detail with their children, there are certain facts that kids of any age need to learn. They should know that income is limited, that some of it must be saved and the rest parcelled out carefully to pay for everyday expenses, big-ticket items and occasional splurges. The money for a meal at McDonald's today may not be available for your family's next summer vacation.

The best way to teach children the financial facts of life is to give them some money of their own to spend, save, invest, fool around with and, yes, waste. That's the purpose of an allowance—to let kids make their own choices and their own mistakes. Later, they can use money from babysitting and summer jobs to practise hands-on financial management.

As parents, we can help demystify the secrets of money and teach children any lessons we have learned along the way. But we also have to be good role models. Our behaviour—not our moralizing—is what kids notice and remember.

For children under 12, research has shown their purchasing acumen has little to do with the size of their weekly allowance. It is more a matter of what their parents do. Kids are copycats. If you are a savvy consumer and never make a purchase without comparison shopping and haggling, that's what your children will emulate. If you are disciplined and save 10 per cent of what you earn, so will your kids. Teenagers, of course, like to rebel against their parents and go their own way. But most eventually revert to the money habits they learned as young children.

In this chapter, I'll talk about some of the big issues involving kids and money—getting an allowance, opening a savings account, investing in stocks and mutual funds, and talking to children about your own finances.

Allowances

When do you start giving an allowance? The best time is when children have acquired some understanding of money and math skills, probably after the age of five. Another sign of readiness is when they watch television, see commercials and demand the products they see. Some kids have a bad case of the "gimmes" and think parents have an unlimited supply of cash. Once they are footing the bill, their wish list contracts dramatically.

How much do you pay? It depends on how mature the child is and what he or she is expected to do with the money. You can ask some of your child's friends or their parents how much they get so you won't be totally out of line. Before deciding on an allowance, decide what expenses it will cover. Parents can set guidelines, along with the children, about what you pay for and what they pay for. Who is responsible for lunch at school, snacks, bus fare, comics or video rentals? If the child wants a $50 pair of jeans and you think a $30 pair is good enough, which one of you should cover the difference?

In my view, an allowance is not meant to reward children for basic chores they do around the house. As responsible family members, they are expected to keep up their share of housework, such as cleaning rooms and making beds. They should not have to be paid for behaviour that is a normal part of cooperative living—and they won't forfeit the money if they fail to perform their duties. Allowances are to be paid unconditionally to children whether they "deserve" it or not. The money is given in an attempt to teach youngsters about spending and saving. It's not a bribe or a punishment.

At the same time, you can offer children the chance to earn more—over and above their basic stipend—for any extra jobs they might undertake. They can wash the family car, polish the silverware, dust the books or find an out-of-the-ordinary job that parents want done and are willing to subsidize. This kind of initiative helps kids get closer to a financial goal, heading off discouragement when saving seems to take too long.

One of the first problems a child quickly confronts is what to do when the money runs out. If the allowance you pay on Sunday is gone by Tuesday, and there are still expenses to cover for the rest of the week, should you give an advance on next week's allowance? Maybe once or twice, but not if this develops into a pattern. If parents are always there to save kids from their financial mistakes, the kids will never learn how to handle money.

Instead, consider lending the money to the child and charging a realistic interest rate. This will reinforce the idea that actions have consequences and profligacy carries penalties. It may sound mean and heartless, but parents have to remember that an allowance is an educational tool. Setting strict limits and refusing emergency bailouts are the lessons you teach and kids learn.

If the money always runs out before the week does, the problem may be that the allowance is no longer adequate for the child's needs. Review the amount every few months to ensure that there is enough for spending and saving, plus a little extra for fun. Encourage kids to ask Mom or Dad for a cost-of-living raise and marshal strong arguments in their favour. This is excellent training in negotiating skills for later life. Remind them that they have to come up with something better than "All my friends get more than I do!"

If a child is six or seven and has no special financial needs, you can start the allowance with a couple of dollars and add a dollar at each birthday. Just as a boss doesn't tell workers how to spend their money, let your child decide what to buy, advises New York therapist Linda Barbanel in a helpful book, *Piggy Bank to Credit Card*. If you don't want the child to overdose on candy bars, discuss this at the outset when you decide on the specifics of the allowance. "Talk about the different kinds of snacks that would be more nutritious," she says. "However, be aware that kids use their discretionary money to buy things you probably frown on, and candy bars fit that category."

Give your child a colourful change purse or wallet to celebrate starting an allowance. Then, make sure there is a special place to store the savings. My mother gave each of her five grandchildren a metal cash box they could lock and keep safe from prying siblings. A bank is a perfect present for this age group, or you can help your child make one from a recycled can or box. The bank should be easy to open so kids can count the change often and see how they're doing.

Hand over change in small denominations to encourage youngsters to save. If an allowance is two dollars, for example, don't give a $2 bill; give a loonie, three quarters, two dimes and a nickel. It's never too soon to get kids into the habit of paying themselves first. Out of each allowance, 10 per cent should be set aside immediately for savings. Two dimes of the two-dollar allowance will go into the bank.

What should the child do with the savings? It's important to set goals together. Without a defined goal, children (and adults too) often lack the discipline to siphon off cash and leave it intact. You might consider setting both short-term goals—such as a special toy or outing in the next few months—and long-term goals—say, a video game or in-line skates.

Make sure the goals are concrete and immediate. Young children have trouble saving for a long-term abstract goal like a university education. A child of six or seven may not be able to plan any further into the future than two or three weeks. By the time they are teenagers, kids' ability to plan for the future is more developed. Children of 13 or 14 can start receiving their allowance every two weeks or monthly. A longer pay period requires more astute financial planning to make the money last. Older children can take responsibility for buying gifts, entertainment and some or all of their clothing.

Some youngsters love to put money aside and hate to spend a penny of their stash. My son Charles is like that. Most of his allowances and cash gifts go into a savings account and investments, and he feels secure knowing the money is there if he needs it. For this type of frugal kid, saving is enough of a goal and there is no need to visualize tangible rewards.

Charitable giving can be part of the allowance too. Some people use the 10 per cent rule (or tithing) for their own donations. Like saving, this is a good habit for parents to instill in kids at a young age.

There are many ways for children to share their wealth. They can give change to homeless people or musicians on the street, support an environmental organization, give to a children's charity such as UNICEF or Ronald McDonald House or a more broadly based campaign such as the United Way, or donate groceries or time to a food drive organized by their school, club church or synagogue.

Don't worry about getting a tax receipt from the charity. Unlike adults, kids are unlikely to need the tax break, and their donations cannot be claimed by their parents, so they can give to a wider range of causes. Let children make their own choices. The more involved they are in picking the charitable organization, the more committed they will be to contributing part of their allowance each week.

Some experts also suggest that "taxes" be taken out of each child's "gross" allowance. You can explain to your child how taxes work in real life, that they go to buy things for the greater good of the whole group, like roads and public libraries. Your "family tax" can be used for the same purpose—to buy something the whole family agrees on and will enjoy, such as a vacation or video game.

Savings Accounts

When do you open a savings account for your child? You might start one when the child is born, but the ideal age is nine or ten, when children are old enough to understand such concepts as deposits and withdrawals, cheques and interest. They are starting to get money gifts that are too big to keep safely at home and they are looking for a haven to keep savings immune from temptation. If they have enough money saved, interest can help them reach a goal a little faster.

To encourage kids to make regular deposits, you may want to consider some sort of incentive plan. For example, you can match the amount they have put aside at the end of each month with equivalent funds.

Before opening an account, talk to your child about saving money in a bank. "Kids have funny ideas of what happens to their money when they hand it over to the teller," says Linda Barbanel. "Some worry that they'll never see it again because it will get mixed up with everybody else's money." Reassure the child that the money won't get lost and can be taken out at any time, and that the bank will record the amount in a passbook or monthly statement.

Talk to your child about interest, a concept that can be tricky for kids to grasp. Explain how banks make money by charging a higher rate to borrowers than they pay to depositors. And teach the difference between simple and compound interest. Emphasize that more frequent compounding of interest allows savers to earn more.

When children know how to multiply and divide, parents can tell them about the rule of 72. Take the rate of interest paid on your savings, divide it into 72 and that is the number of years it will take for your money to double. At 6 per cent interest, your money takes 12 years to double. At 9 per cent, it takes eight years. This rule helps kids understand interest rates in a more concrete way.

If a child is worried about losing money, you can allay those fears by pointing out that the government guarantees the return of funds if a financial institution collapses. The Canada Deposit Insurance Corp., backed by a line of credit from the federal treasury, insures depositors against losses of up to $60,000. Point out the CDIC decal on a bank's window or door.

When opening a child's account, it's convenient to stay with the same institution that has your money. But remember that kids' accounts are not tamper-proof. Financial institutions have the right to use children's money to cover any shortfalls or money owing on parents' accounts. So if that's a possibility, it may be best to keep the kids' savings elsewhere to avoid this potential conflict.

Shop around for the best deal. Banks, trust companies and credit unions are all courting young savers with preferential interest rates and few or no service charges. They know customers develop long-term relationships with financial institutions and each wants to be first in line.

Among the goodies you can get are free piggy banks, rulers, pencil cases and discounts on children's magazines. Some financial institutions give free cheques and access to automatic teller machines if parents agree. Most have excellent booklets on banking and money management for kids. (You can also get good educational materials from the Canadian Bankers Association, Box 1500, Station A, Toronto, Ont. M5W 2N8.)

As a working parent, what matters most to me is the branch location and hours of business. The branch should make it convenient for you and your child to visit. Charles recently switched his account from a bank that observed "banker's hours" to a trust company that stayed open late in the evening and all day Saturday. Now, I can accompany him to the branch, impossible before because I was always at the office.

Another consideration is the minimum amount needed to buy a guaranteed investment certificate. Some financial institutions want as little as $100, while others require $500 to $1,000. Savings accounts pay next to nothing and kids can earn a premium interest rate by saving for the longer term with a GIC. But the minimum should be reasonable, so they can attain it easily.

Here are some questions that children can ask a financial institution about a savings account:

- How much money do I need to open an account?
- Do I need a certain amount to make a deposit?

- Are there are any monthly fees? If so, how are they paid?
- How much interest do you pay and how often? When do I get it?
- Can the interest rate change at any time? Will I be notified?
- How do I get money out of the account? Can I go to another branch of the same institution?
- What happens if I lose my passbook?
- Are there any other services available to me, such as telephone banking and access to automated teller machines?

Children should try to make regular deposits and watch the money grow. After a few months, when interest appears in the passbook, there will be a further incentive to save—especially if you let them spend the interest once in a while. Parents should talk up the idea of saving at every opportunity, so the child does not treat the bank account as another hobby or toy, given total attention for two weeks and then forgotten.

Investments

At the age when kids are ready to open a savings account, they can also start thinking about taking some risk with their money to make it grow. A 10-year-old isn't too young to be introduced to stocks, even if he or she would rather trade baseball cards or scratch-and-smell stickers than Inco or Alcan shares.

Kids will learn more from risky investments than from safe ones. As Toronto financial planner Chris Snyder says in his book *How to Teach Your Children About Money:* "The sooner children are exposed to uncertain ventures, the less they will fear them. People who never take risks may attach excessive importance to money and security. That would be an unhealthy perspective, not to be encouraged in children."

Sometimes, grandparents start children on an investing program. My late grandmother would give us single shares of Bell Telephone (now BCE Inc.) for birthdays and special occasions. My three brothers and I loved getting dividend cheques every few months, and by the time we reached adulthood, we had a nice legacy. (I cashed in my shares a while ago to subsidize taking a few months off work.)

As parents, we can suggest to grandparents and other relatives that they give financial presents to our kids instead of toys and games or clothes. Kids hooked on the latest fashion trend may not appreciate a financial gift when they're young, but they will in the future. Stocks and mutual funds last longer and rarely go out of style.

Stocks

We can also start our own investing program and get the children involved. A favourite strategy is to buy one, five or ten shares of a company the child chooses. Certain stocks have kid appeal because their products are popular with small fry. Examples are Disney, Coca-Cola, Toys "Я" Us, McDonald's, all traded in the U.S., or Canadian Tire, Canstar Sports (which makes hockey gear) and Cinram (which makes compact discs) in Canada.

Some publicly traded companies really cater to young shareholders. Investors in Walt Disney Co. become members in the Magic Kingdom Club and get discounts of 10 to 30 per cent on Disney resorts and hotels. Irwin Toy's junior shareholder program gives special share certificates and pamphlets explaining investment terms, and its annual meeting attracts legions of youngsters who get to try out the toys.

But stocks with kid appeal are not always the best investments. Some pay no dividends and others have experienced steep price declines. Irwin Toy, for example, loses money in years when its products fall out of favour and its price reflects this mixed profit history. I bought Irwin Toy shares for Charles at $8 apiece in February 1992. Today, the stock is $7.00. At the same time, I bought Canadian Tire at $19.87. Threatened by U.S. competitor Wal-Mart, it has since slipped to $11.

Better for your kids' nerves—and your own—is to choose companies that provide an essential service and are virtually recession-proof, such as banks, telephone companies, and gas and electric utilities. These are "blue-chip" stocks, with lots of shareholders, stable profits, low volatility, high dividend yields and a history of increasing their dividends over the years. The shares of Bank of Nova Scotia I bought at $21 apiece in 1992 are now $27. (They were as high as $33 early in 1994.) Kids can relate to banks, especially if they have just opened a savings account at one. Talk to kids about the wisdom of owning a piece of the company they patronize as a customer.

Explain that the dividend yield on bank stocks, averaging 4 to 5 per cent, is competitive with short-term interest rates—and that's before including the tax break on dividends. Canada's major banks have treated shareholders well, better than they have treated depositors, and their stocks are perennial investor favourites.

Many blue-chip stocks offer a dividend reinvestment program. This means that instead of getting quarterly dividend cheques in the mail, you allocate the money to buy more shares. This is a good way to get stock without paying any commissions, especially if the company lets you contribute extra amounts (beyond the reinvested dividends) to the program. Most do.

Commissions—the fees you pay to stockbrokers for executing trades—can be a major irritant when investing for children. If you buy one share of a company for, say, $20, you may have to pay $50 or more in commissions. The brokerage costs are quite high on a small number of shares.

You can cut commission costs by using a discount broker, a no-frills firm that does trading but provides no research or advice. Most big banks have their own discount brokerage operations. The minimum commission is about $30 for each trade, and you pay an extra fee to register the shares in the child's name. Don't expect to have a relationship with a discount broker. You deal with a different person each time you call.

Another way to cut costs is to attend the Financial Forum, a free investor event held each February in Toronto and Vancouver. The Toronto Stock Exchange sets up a mini-exchange where you can buy shares of about a dozen companies at a nominal commission, usually a flat $10 for 10 shares or fewer. Many stocks sold at the forum have dividend reinvestment programs.

Also of interest to kids is the Young Investors Club set up in 1992 by Odlum Brown, a Vancouver investment dealer. The way it works is that a parent, relative or family friend buys the securities, which are registered in the child's name. (The young investor doesn't actually have an account at the brokerage.) Members get semi-annual newsletters with stock ideas, games and tips. Two versions are produced, one for younger kids and one for teenagers. For information, write to Young Investors Club, c/o Odlum Brown, 1800 – 609 Granville St., P.O. Box 10012, Vancouver, B.C. V7Y 1A3, telephone (604) 844-5317.

Mutual Funds

Mutual funds are popular investments for children. With a mutual fund, you pool your money with other investors to get a share of a portfolio holding 50, 100 or 200 stocks. By spreading your money over more companies, you get greater diversification and lower risk than if you bought stocks on your own. Another advantage of mutual funds is that your money is managed by professionals. This is a relief for busy people. You don't have to follow the stock market every day and agonize over when to buy and sell—the portfolio manager does it for you.

You can get into a mutual fund with a small stake of $100 to $500. If you want to add money regularly you can go as low as $50 a month. The concept is perfect for the small investor. And you don't have to ask if you can reinvest the dividends in new fund shares: it's done automatically for you.

However, choosing a fund can be confusing. In the past few years, the mutual fund industry has boomed and the number of choices has exploded to 1,000 or so, with a dizzying array of investment objectives. Unlike high-profile company stocks, mutual funds do not have names that ring a bell with children—or with most adults, for that matter. Probably the best known are Templeton, Mackenzie and Altamira, companies that advertise a lot and have achieved impressive results over the years.

When comparing funds, look for one with a track record of at least five years. It should have low volatility and consistent above-average returns. Avoid funds with spectacular short-term results, since the managers are probably taking a lot of risk to get those high numbers. The star performer this year may be next year's dog.

Your child can call or write to several mutual fund companies for a prospectus and annual report. Check to see if the material is clearly presented and easy to read, not written for someone with an advanced business degree. Look at what is in the portfolio and who is in charge. The company should be able to tell you how long the same person or team has been managing the fund and whether they are responsible for achieving the past results.

A good book for beginners is Gordon Pape's *Buyer's Guide to Mutual Funds,* published annually. Mr. Pape, a Toronto author and broadcaster, rates mutual funds like movies, on a scale of one to four (he uses $ signs instead of stars), and his capsule comments make easy reading for kids 10 and older. The book usually hits the shelves in late fall.

Mutual funds are available from a number of sources—stockbrokers, banks, trust companies, credit unions, life insurance agents, financial planners and directly from the fund managers in some cases. One of the first decisions you have to make is whether to buy a front load, back load or no load fund.

With a front load fund, you pay a commission or sales charge when you make your purchase. With a back load, or deferred sales charge, fund, you pay the commission when you sell—but the longer you hold on, the lower the charge. If you hold on for at least five years, the commission may disappear altogether.

When you buy a no load fund, you pay nothing to buy, sell or switch from one fund to another. No load funds are sold by salaried bank and trust company staff or by people who work directly for the mutual fund distributor. They can tell you about the funds they sell, but they are not trained to survey the entire marketplace and tell you which funds are the best for your needs. Shopping around to compare prices and performance is your responsibility.

Load funds are sold by independent salespeople, who earn up-front commissions and ongoing fees from the mutual fund managers. If you want impartial advice and help in choosing a fund, you might want to work with an intermediary. But make sure you are getting good service that is worth what you are paying for it.

Every mutual fund, whether load or no load, charges a management fee. This covers investment advice, trading costs, advertising, legal work and so on. The money is taken directly from the fund's assets each year. The published performance results are what you get *after* the deduction of management fees.

What kind of mutual fund should you buy? If kids are young and can invest their money for a number of years, stock funds are the way to go. Stock prices go up and down unpredictably, but patient investors usually do well over the long run. You can choose a Canadian, U.S. or international fund, or an ethical or environmental fund.

For children who have more immediate needs for their money and little appetite for risk, a balanced fund is the best bet. These funds combine stocks with bonds and treasury bills to lessen the up-and-down swings. Again, there is a large selection of U.S. and international balanced funds as well as Canadian ones.

Whether you buy stocks or mutual funds, encourage your child to follow their progress regularly. Together, you can scan the business pages of the newspaper to see how your investments are doing—not every day, but periodically—and read the quarterly or annual reports. If the price is sagging, you can discuss whether to sell or hold on.

It's no fun to lose money, even on paper, and children may find it particularly troubling. Without experience in investing, they don't understand that stocks and mutual funds can plummet in price and shoot back up again. They probably have less patience than you do and will be more eager to dump a loser instead of waiting till it turns around.

But mutual funds are long-term investments, and you should be prepared to hold a fund for three to five years. (That's why it's silly to follow the price every day. Once a month is probably enough.) If your fund starts lagging behind the competition, give the manager a chance to get back on track. Eventually, most hot funds cool off and losers turn into winners again. By the time you spot the top performers, they are probably past their peak and ready to head down again.

But sometimes, you have to yield to a child's discomfort and sell a losing investment—even if you disagree.

Dummy Portfolios

If your child has little stomach for risk—or if you feel the same—one way to toughen up is to put together a dummy, or phantom, portfolio. You pretend you have a certain amount of money to invest, say $10,000, and pick several stocks or mutual funds. Follow their progress over a year and see how your choices do. To make the "virtual reality" experiment more exciting, parents can offer to pay children the amount of the gain in the shares over that period.

A dummy portfolio allows first-time investors to be more adventurous. You can add some long shots to the mix, along with more conservative choices, to see the difference in return. With no real money on the line, you can have fun, follow your hunches and develop a feel for how the stock market works.

Talking to Your Children about Money

Charles would love to know how much money his parents make. He asks us all the time, and we never tell him. (Richard is still too young to care.) But like many people, we keep this information close to our vests and don't trust our kids not to blurt it out to others. Exactly how much we earn is no one's business but our own (and our accountant's).

In talking to your children about money, you don't have to bare your soul or admit all your mistakes. "I do not believe that your child needs to know that you once bounced seven cheques in one day, or that you were denied a mortgage four times before finally getting one," says Neale S. Godfrey, chair of the Children's Financial Network in the United States and author of *Money Doesn't Grow on Trees: A Parent's Guide to Raising Financially Responsible Children*.

However, there is some information that older children, and certainly teenagers, need to be aware of for their own benefit. It concerns the financial planning you and your spouse have done for the future. In particular, they should know about the arrangements you have made to protect them if you have a serious accident or die unexpectedly.

Talking to kids about this subject without scaring or overwhelming them will demand all your skills and sensitivities as a parent. You can sense when a child is ready to hear what you have to say. Sometimes, an opportunity presents itself when a youngster starts asking questions about death. From the age of four or five, this is a major source of curiosity.

Children realize how dependent they are on their parents and wonder what will happen to them if you die. As long as you have an up-to-date will, you can reassure them that you have provided for them to be loved and taken care of by someone else. They will not be put out on the street.

"Your child already knows that you plan carefully ahead of time who will take care of him after school if you're not there, on Saturday nights if you go out, and if you and your spouse go out of town together on business or a vacation," says Ms. Godfrey. "Explain that a will is just an extension of that same kind of planning." A young child needs to hear that the plan will probably not be used until you are very old and he or she is grown up. It is there just in case of emergency. You can show an older child where you keep the document and spell out some of the details. The same applies to a power of attorney form.

If you and your spouse both carry life insurance, explain to the children that this money will help support them if something happens to either parent. An older child can be told where the policies are kept, who are the insurance agents and what companies they represent. Kids should also know who to contact in an emergency.

By the time your children reach the age of seven or eight, you can show them if there is a special drawer, file cabinet or locked box in the home or office where you keep important financial records. These might include:

- Information relating to your bank accounts, such as your passbook or monthly statements.
- The location of your safety-deposit box and keys.
- The names of your lawyer, accountant and financial advisors.
- Your investment documents, such as stock certificates, Canada Savings Bonds, government bonds, GICs and mutual fund prospectuses, as well as monthly statements from a stockbroker or mutual fund dealer.

- Annual statements relating to your RRSPs, government retirement programs and your employers' pension plans.
- Your car insurance and home insurance policies, with the agents' names and telephone numbers.
- An inventory of your household contents. This is crucial to making an insurance claim if there is a fire or theft.
- Supplementary health or insurance benefits from an employer, union or voluntary association.
- The deed to your house and any other properties you own.
- Birth and marriage certificates and any documents relating to separation or divorce.
- Details about your mortgages and consumer loans.
- A list of your credit card accounts in case your wallet is stolen. A quick way to compile this is to empty your wallet and photocopy the cards.
- Tax returns going back for the last three to five years.

If you have any valuable possessions—such as jewellery, furs or art—your older children should know where they are. Do you have an emergency fund or wad of cash hidden away somewhere? Keep a record of it with your papers. Also, make sure the kids can locate your personal address book.

Obviously, if you are disorganized and keep documents all over the place, you will have to make an effort to put them together. This is for the benefit of your spouse as well as your kids. A cardboard or plastic accordion file works well. Insurance agents can provide booklets to record personal information. You can also keep a list of vital names and numbers on your home computer, as long as you're not the only one in the family who knows how to operate it.

Children should know if their parents are saving for their education through a registered education savings plan or another type of account. If there is money set aside in a college fund, kids may feel more secure about their future and more motivated to stay in school. This is especially important with an RESP, because the earnings will be confiscated if your child becomes a high-school dropout. So, tell them and tell them and tell them again.

It's vital to talk to and involve the children if there is a major change in your financial circumstances. This can be a bad thing (a job loss, layoff or cut in pay) or a good thing (an inheritance, promotion or raise). Either way, kids should know about any impending shifts in their standard of living.

Since the onset of the 1990 recession, many families have slashed their expenses. Some parents lost their jobs and took lower-paid positions. Others started their own businesses and learned to live with pay fluctuations. Even those who kept their jobs and salaries were hit with higher taxes and declining real incomes.

If you are facing a financial setback, talk to your children about what they can do to help. Kids want to help because it makes them feel more in control and needed, says Neale Godfrey. Perhaps a child can suspend his or her allowance and donate it toward the family's support, organize a garage sale or take on extra household jobs. Youngsters can be helpful in a family emergency, so parents should mobilize their energy and support.

Involve the children in your decision-making and your efforts to cut back spending. Challenge them to come up with ways to save money, say on groceries or utilities, and offer to share the savings with them. Get them to calculate the difference between brand names and generic products and ask if they are willing to switch. Figure out how much you can save by buying in bulk.

At the dinner table and on car trips, family members can have spirited discussions about money and how they feel about it. Here are suggested topics of conversation from Paula

Hogan, a Milwaukee financial planner, in the *Journal of the American Association of Individual Investors:*

- What increased responsibility should kids in our family get each year?
- When are kids in our family expected to become financially independent? When did each parent become financially independent?
- What would each of us do if we won $1 million in a lottery? What should the government do with an extra $1 million? Should the government be in the lottery business?
- Are there some things that money can't buy?
- What are the different attitudes toward money within our own family?
- What makes someone a saver, a spendthrift or indifferent to money?
- What are luxuries? What are necessities to us that would be luxuries to others? If we were hit with some kind of financial hardship, what could we live without and not live without?
- When the parents were growing up, how much financial help did they get from their parents—for example, in going to school, setting up an apartment or buying a first home? What are the pros and cons of parents helping older children?
- What are some mistakes that the parents made in earlier years with respect to money? Which mistakes should a parent not let a child make?

If you work with children to teach financial responsibility, you eventually realize that letting kids make mistakes is not only okay, it is the main goal. At first, letting children order junk from a catalogue, make inappropriate impulse purchases or spend their whole allowance on candy can feel strange. But blowing $10 when you're nine is a great way to learn *not* to blow $10,000 when you're 30.

A child's mistakes also provide a good opportunity for parents to share their own bloopers, reinforcing the notion that "we're all in this together," says Paula Hogan.

Another important result of handing over money decisions is a shift in the relationship between parent and child. Children who have clear and gradually expanding boundaries within which they are free to manage money tend to stop begging for more money or more treats. If they know they have a piece of turf to manage in their own way, they try hard to figure out how best to use their resources.

I saw the ground shift myself while walking with my son Richard, then seven, through a Price Club store. He was nagging me to buy him something, I can't remember what, and I had said no repeatedly. But he kept up the onslaught. Finally, I told him he could buy it if he paid for the purchase himself. He started to cry, realizing the money would have to come out of his well-stuffed piggy bank and not wanting to spend it. He never asked for anything again in the course of that shopping trip.

So, as your child goes from nagging you for candy to comparing the prices and sizes of different chocolate bars, heave a sigh of relief. It's a sign of maturity when kids learn to make financial choices and manage money sensibly. Our role is not to tell them what to do with their money but to set limits and boundaries. They have to trim their desires to fit the parameters we assign.

Does this sound familiar? Being a parent is about setting limits and teaching kids to make choices in all spheres of life. Handling money is no different from the other important lessons kids absorb on the road to becoming responsible adults. They have to make their own mistakes. And we have to watch and smile (through our tears and gritted teeth) as they learn from failure.

BIBLIOGRAPHY

Barbanel, Linda, *Piggy Bank to Credit Card* (Crown, New York), $13.00.

Berg, Adrianne G., *Making up for Lost Time: Speed Investing for a Secure Future* (Hearst Books, U.S.A.), $32.95.

Bullock, James, and Brett, George, *Insure Sensibly: A Guide to Life and Disability Insurance* (Penguin, Toronto), $14.99.

Canadian Personal Tax Planning Guide, KPMG Peat Marwick Thorne (Carswell, Toronto), $14.95.

Cochrane, Michael, *Surviving Divorce: The Everyday Guide to Canadian Family Law* (Prentice-Hall, Toronto), $16.95.

Coulter, Laurie, *Two Houses: A Parent's Guide to Joint Custody in Canada* (Harper Collins, Toronto), $17.95.

Estess, Patricia Schiff, *Remarriage and Your Money: Once Again for Richer or Poorer* (Little, Brown, New York), $24.95.

Flynn, Donald, *The Truth About Funerals* (Funeral Consultants International, Toronto), $16.95.

Godfrey, Neale S., *Money Doesn't Grow on Trees: A Parent's Guide to Raising Financially Responsible Children* (Simon & Schuster, New York), $14.00.

Jordan, Dorothy, and Cohen, Marjorie Adoff, *Great Vacations with Your Kids* (Family Digest, New York), $2.25.

Kerr, Robert, *The Only Retirement Guide You'll Ever Need* (Penguin, Toronto), $19.99.

MacFarlane, Lynne, *Double Income Families* (Key Porter, Toronto), $18.95.

Martorana, R. George, and Rowland, Susan, "*Your Pension and Your Spouse*", Canadian edition (International Foundation of Employee Benefit Plans, Wisconsin).

Matthews, Betsy, and Birch, Richard, *Taking Care of Tomorrow: The Canadian Money Book for Prime Time Women* (McGraw-Hill Ryerson, Toronto), $17.95.

Pape, Gordon, *1995 Buyer's Guide to Mutual Funds* (Prentice-Hall, Toronto), $14.95.

Payne, Julien and Marilyn, *Dealing with Family Law: A Canadian Guide* (McGraw-Hill Ryerson, Toronto), $12.95.

——, Engel, Marjorie L. and Gould, Diana D., *The Canadian Divorce Decisions Workbook* (McGraw-Hill Ryerson, Toronto), $26.95.

Reynolds, Nancy Thalia, *Adopting Your Child: Options, Answers and Actions* (Self-Counsel Press, Toronto), $12.95.

Rhodes, Ann, *The Eldercare Sourcebook* (Key Porter, Toronto), $18.95.

Rodgers, Kelly, *The Insider's Guide to Choosing the Best Money Manager* (Rodgers Investment Consulting, Toronto), $19.95.

Snyder, Christopher, *How to Teach Your Children About Money* (now out of print).

Wade, P.J. *Have Your Home and Money Too* (John Wiley & Sons, Toronto), $16.95.

West, Michelle, *Seniority: In Search of the Best Nursing Homes and Alternative Care in Canada* (now out of print).

INDEX

A

accommodation,
for children 141
Adopting Your Child: Options, Answers and Actions 132
adoption 131-33
Adoption in Canada 132
advance health care directive 73, 74
aging and death, discussion of 96-97
"aging in place" 108
AIDS, and your will 27-28
air travel, with children 140-41
Alberta:
financial planners in 119
Students Finance Board 167
Alberta Camping Association 135
"Alimony or Maintenance" (Revenue Canada) 52
alimony, and taxation 38
allowances, for children 176-80
alternative accommodation 108
American Association of Individual Investors, Journal 194
annuities 21-22
annuity-based reverse mortgage 104-105
assets:
and common-law spouse 12
and family law 5
location of 99
and marriage contracts 6
pension plan 45-46
Association des Camps du Québec 135
Associations of Universities and Colleges of Canada 168
attribution rules 16-17

B

baby bonus 149, 155
babysitters 126
back load mutual funds 188
balanced mutual funds 188-89
bank accounts:
and separation 34
signing authority 42
bank insurance, vs. life insurance 81-82
Bank of Nova Scotia 185

bankruptcy 35, 50-51
banks, and children 181
Barbanel, Linda 178, 181
"bed and breakfast" establishments:
  and retirement 103
  and travel with children 142-43
beneficiary, designations 41
benefits 17-20
  payment of 131
Berg, Adriane G. 96, 98
Birch, Richard 32
blended families 52-57
borrowing power 61
Brett, George 78, 87, 88, 161
British Columbia Camping Association 135
British Columbia, Student Services Branch 167
Brown, Odlum 186
bulk buying, as saving strategy 145-46
Bullock, James 78, 84, 87, 88, 161
business:
  assets 7
  income 15
  and marriage contracts 43
  and your will 27
business equipment, and insurance 91
buy-sell agreements 27
Buyer's Guide to Mutual Funds (Pape) 187

C

camp:
  checklist for 134-35
  choosing 133-36
Camping Association of Nova Scotia 136
camping, as family holiday 143
Canada Deposit Insurance Corp. (CDIC) 81, 152, 181
Canada Life 160
Canada Mortgage and Housing Corp. 105
  and low-cost housing for elderly 108
Canada Pension Plan *See* CPP
Canada Savings Bonds, for emergency funds 64
Canada Student Loans Program 166-67
Canada-U.S. tax treaty 107-108
Canadian Association of Financial Planners 32, 120
Canadian Automobile Association 138
Canadian Bankers Association 182
Canadian Bond Rating Service 80
Canadian Camping Association 135
Canadian Divorce Decisions Workbook, The 35
Canadian Hospital Association (CHA) 108
Canadian Hospital Directory (CHD) 108
Canadian Life and Health Compensation Corp. (CompCorp) 81
Canadian Life and Health Insurance Association 75, 83, 84, 138
Canadian Medical Association 73
Canadian Personal Tax Planning Guide, The (KPMG Peat Marwick Thorne) 16, 130
Canadian Scholarship Trust 150
Canadian Tire 184, 185
cancer, and your will 27-28
Canstar Sports 184
capital cost allowance 169
capital gain:

investing for 157
and living trusts 163-64
capital gains tax 12-13, 97
at death 99-100, 117
principal residence exemption 12-13, 53
RESPs 155
car travel, with children 139-40
cash value insurance policies 77-78
cat owners, insurance for 92-93
Centre for Bioethics 74
charitable donations, and unmarried couples 12
charitable giving, and allowances 180
charitable remainder trust 164
Charter of Rights, and same-sex couples 10-11
Chartered Financial Consultant (Ch.F.C.) 80, 120
Chartered Financial Planner (C.F.P.) 120
Chartered Life Underwriter (C.L.U.) 80
child care:
division of labour 7
expense deduction 12
hiring 126-31
tax-deductible, rules for 129-30
child support 37-38
custody arrangement 46-47
and divorce 31-32
enforcement of 33, 51
and insurance 40
modifying 54
payment 40-41, 50
See also spousal support
child tax benefit 12, 14, 51-52, 155
children:
and common-law couples 9-10
cost of raising 125-26
and financial acumen 176-80
investing earnings of 163
and marriage contracts 7-8
new, in second marriages 54-56
and savings 155-56
and taxation 131, 155, 157-58
and your will 26-27
Children's Education Trust of Canada 150
Children's Financial Network 190
C.I.M. (Certified Investment Management), 120
Cinram 184
co-op programs 168-69
Coca-Cola 184
Cochrane, Michael 6-7, 8, 9-10, 36, 45, 48, 50
cohabitation agreements 8-10
Cohen, Marjorie Adoff 136, 137, 144
collateral:
house as 62
and RRSPs 63
commission costs 185-86
common-law couples:
and health insurance 18
and house insurance 91-92
and taxes 11-13
and visitation rights 48
and wills 27-28
common-law spouse:
and financial support 37
and pension rights 22
and property rights 8-9
and taxation 51
communication links, for elderly 108
compounding, and RRSPs 173
Compulife Software 80
Concerned Friends of Ontario Citizens in Care Facilities 110
condominium, rental and travel 142
constructive trust 44-45

Consumer Reports magazine 114
control, and money issues 3
Corbin, Barry 66, 72
cottage rental 143
Coulter, Laurie 47, 48
counselling, and visitation rights 49-50
couples:
  and money management 1-2
  non-romantic, and property rights 10
court orders 48
CPP (Canada Pension Plan) 15, 17
  death benefits 115
  pension-splitting 45-46
CPP/QPP (Canada Pension Plan/Quebec Pension Plan), pension-splitting 45-46
credit cards:
  for emergency funds 63
  and insurance promotions 85
  and separation 34
credit counselling service 34-35
Cullis, Tara 2
custody 46-49

D

day camp 133-34
day care 126-27
Dealing with Family Law: A Canadian Guide (Payne) 37
death:
  and children 190-91
  and support obligations 41, 51
death benefits 24
  Canada Pension Plan 115
deferred sales charge mutual funds 188
defined benefit plan 20-21
defined contribution plan 21
Delaney, Tom 156
Delta Hotels 141
depreciated value, insurance 90-91
Directory of Long-Term Care Centres in Canada (CHA) 108
disability credit 111
"Disability Insurance: Where Will the Money Come From If You're Disabled?" (CLHIA) 84
disability insurance 19-20, 83-89
  and blended families 54
  and child support 51
  gender differences 88
  questions to ask 86-87
discount brokers 85-86
dividend tax credit 157
divorce:
  and family law 5
  mediation 36-37
  and your will 25
Divorce Act (1985) 36, 47, 48
dog owners, insurance for 92
domestic contract *See* marriage contracts
Dominion Bond Rating Service 80
Double Income Families (MacFarlane) 2
double-income families, and taxation 13
Drache, Arthur 122
durable power of attorney 71
Dying with Dignity 74

E

education:
  of children 7-8, 9
  funds 54
  post-secondary, cost of 147-48
Eldercare Sourcebook, The 108
elderly, and inheritance 117

emergency:
  fund 192
  preparing for 60-64
employee assistance programs, and elder care 109
employer, benefits payable 130-31
enduring power of attorney 71
equal contributions, and money management 3
equity funds, investing in 157
equivalent-to-spouse tax credit 12-13
equivalent-to-spouse tax deduction 51
"estate freeze" 100
estate planning 42, 98-102
  and blended families 55
  and your parents 97
  See also taxation
Estess, Patricia Schiff 52, 53, 55, 56
Everyday Guide to Canadian Family Law, The (Cochrane) 36
executor:
  choosing a 67-68
  and funeral plans 113
  trust company as 122-23

F

"family assets", definition of 43
family, blended 53-58
family income, tax disparities 13-14
Family Law Act (Ontario) (1986) and marriage contracts 43-44
family law (provincial) 5
family property, division of 43-46
family service associations, and housing for elderly 109
Family Travel Times 144
F.C.S.I. (Fellow of the Canadian Securities Institute) 120
Federal Court of Appeal 38
fee-based manager 121
Financial Forum 186
financial issues:
  and children 56, 125-26, 196-95
  in relationships 2
financial planners 110, 119-21
financial records, location of 99, 191-92
financial support 37-42
  after divorce 7
  and common-law unions 9
first to die policy 79-80
"floater" policy 90
Flynn, Donald 112, 113, 115
Fortune magazine 35
Freedman, Janet 16, 128
freelance at home 127
front load mutual fund 188
funerals 112-16
  areas of conflict 113
  prepayment of 115

G

Gibb, Colleen 13
Gibb-Clark, Margot 18
Globe and Mail 18
Godfrey, Neale S. 190-91, 193
grandparents:
  and investing for children 184
  and visitation rights 48-50
"granny flats" 102
Great Vacations with Your Kids (Jordon and Cohen) 136
Great-West Life Assurance 86
group accident and sickness insurance 85
group health insurance plan 138
group life insurance 82
group RRSPs 20-21
GST (goods and services tax) credit 13, 170

Guaranteed Income Supplement 111
guaranteed life insurance plan 114
guardian, choosing a 66-67

H

Harris, Marlys 77
Have Your Home and Money Too (Wade) 105
health aids, for elderly 108
health benefits *See* benefits
health care power of attorney 102
health insurance 18-20
 and family holidays 138-39
Heritage Scholarship Trust 150
Hogan, Paula 193-94
Holiday Inn 141
holidays:
 family 136-45
 package 144
 theme parks 144-45
"holograph" will 68-69
home care:
 for children 126
 for elderly 108
home insurance policy, coverage under 91-92
"Home Insurance and You!" (IBC) 91
home, working at 128
homemakers, and taxation 15
"Hot 100: A Guide to What the Feds Are Doing for Youth" 166
house:
 as financial asset 61
 insurance 88-92
 in remarriage 53
 selling the 106-108
 and separation 43-45
 See also property
household chores, division of labour 7
housing:
 for senior citizens 102, 108-09
 for students 169-70
How to Teach Your Children About Money (Snyder) 183
Howard Johnson 141
Howes, Marie 172
Human Resources Canada 52
human rights laws, and same-sex couples 10-11

I

IAMAT (International Association for Medical Assistance to Travellers) 139
income, for emergency 60-64
income splitting 13-15
 CPP 17
 and living trusts 163-64
 spousal RRSPs 15
income tax:
 installments and disability 83
 and support payments 39-40
Income Tax Act (amendment 1993) 11
Income Tax Act, and tax-free rollover to RRSPs 43-44
incorporation, and pension plans 22
indexed pensions 24
inheritance:
 dealing with 116-23
 managing of 119
 and same-sex couples 10
 taxes 116
 and unmarried couples 10
 without a will 65-66
inherited wealth 118
Insider's Guide to Choosing the Best Money Manager, The (Rodgers) 121
insurance:
 and blended families 54
 pet 92-93
 on retirement 24

travel and health 138-39
insurance broker, how to choose 80-81
Insurance Bureau of Canada 89, 91
insurance policies, and separation 33-34
Insurance Quote Services of Canada 80
insurance trust 40
Insure Sensibly: A Guide to Life and Disability Insurance (Bullock and Brett) 78, 161
"inter vivos" trust 163-64
interest:
income 17
rule of 72 181
investment counsellors 119-21
investment holding company 100
investment income, and income splitting 17-18
investments:
and children 183-84
and cohabitation agreements 9
IPP (individual pension plan) 22
irrevocable beneficiary, of insurance 40
Irwin Toy 184-85

J

joint accounts 42, 100-101
and divorce 31-32
joint and second to die insurance 79
joint custody 46-49
joint and survivor pensions 22-23
"joint tenants with right of survivorship" 28
Jordon, Dorothy 136, 137, 144

K

Kerr, Robert 103, 106, 107
KPMG Peat Marwick Thorne (Toronto) 5, 16, 130, 169

L

lawyers:
cost of 45
and documentation needed 33
and marriage contracts 6-7
need for 35-36
and wills 69-72
legal aid 35
life expectancy, and inheritance 117
life insurance 19, 24
and blended families 54
buying 74-83
and child support 40
estimating need 75-77
and funeral costs 113
as savings vehicle 160-61
LIFE TRAC Report 80
line of credit 62
reverse mortgage 104
live-in help 127-28
"living benefits" 85
living trust 163-64
living wills 72-74, 102
load mutual funds 188
loans:
and disability protection 85
and separation 34
for students 165-68
long-term care, expense of 110-11
long-term disability policies 86
lump sum payments, for support 38

M

MacFarlane, Lynne 2, 3
Magic Kingdom Club 184

maintenance payments, and taxation 38
Making Up for Lost Time: Speed Investing for a Secure Future (Berg) 96
management fee, mutual funds 188
Manitoba:
  and living wills 73
  Ministry of Agriculture 125
  and pension law 45
  Student Aid Branch 167
Manitoba Camping Association 135
marriage contracts 5-8
  provincial jurisdiction 8
  and second marriages 2, 99
  and wills 26
marriage and remarriage:
  and blended families 52-57
  contracts 53
  and money 2
  wills 25-26, 98-100
Martorana, R. George 22
Matthews, Betsy 32
mediation:
  children and grandparents 49-50
  divorce 36-37
mediators, how to find 36
medical expenses, and taxation 12, 18-19, 111
Memorial Society Association of Canada 116
men, changing role of, as providers 2-3
Money Doesn't Grow on Trees: A Parent's Guide to Raising Financially Responsible Children (Godfrey) 190
money issues:
  control and power 3
  and emotions 3
  and remarriages 52-54
  talking about 96, 175, 190-95
Money magazine 77
money management:
  and children 190-95
  five approaches to 3-4
  saving on daily expenses 145-47
money purchase plan 21
mortgage insurance 81-82
mortgages:
  and disability insurance 85
  and family house 44, 61-62
  paying off 162-63
  reverse 103-106
  and separation 34
moving:
  and child support 50
  expense 171
mutual funds:
  investing in 157-59
  as investments for children 186-87
  and RESPs 152

N

nanny 126
  live-out 127, 130
New Brunswick Camping Association 136
New Brunswick, Student Financial Support Services 167
New York Times 118
Newfoundland:
  and intestacy rules 65
  Student Aid Division 167
Newfoundland and Labrador Camping Association 136
Nightingale, Kevyn 169
Nixon, Richard 73
no load mutual funds 188
Northwest Territories:
  and common-law unions 9
  Student Services 168
Norwich Union Life of Toronto 114
Nova Scotia:
  and living wills 73
  Student Assistance

Division 167
"Nursing Home Checklist" 109-10
Nuschke, Michael 117

O

OAS (Old Age Security) 5, 17, 111
Onassis, Jacqueline Kennedy 73
Only Retirement Guide You'll Ever Need, The (Kerr) 103
Ontario:
  automatic wage deduction plan 50
  and intestacy rules 65
  and living wills 73
  probate fees 98
  Students Awards Branch 167
Ontario Camping Association 134, 135
Ontario Family Law Act (1986), and marriage contracts 43-44
overnight camp 133-34

P

package holidays 143-44
Pape, Gordon 187
parents:
  as dependents 110-12
  and need for care 108-10
  in old age 95
part-time work 129
Paul Revere Life Insurance 86
payments, lump sum 38
Payne, Julien and Marilyn 37
pension plans 20-25, 45-46
pension rights, and legal spouse 22
pension splitting 45-46
permanent insurance 77, 79, 82
pet insurance 92-93
Pet Plan 92
Piggy Bank to Credit Card (Barbanel) 178
poverty, and children 32
power of attorney 42, 71-72, 101-102
  possible abuse of 72, 101-102
power, and money issues 3
preferred beneficiary election 164
prenuptial agreement *See* marriage contracts
prepayment penalties, mortgages 61-62
Price Club 145, 195
Prince Edward Island:
  and intestacy rules 65
  Student Aid Division 167
principal residence exemption, capital gains tax 12-13, 53
probate fees 98
Profiling Canada's Families (Vanier) 52, 126
property:
  joint tenancy 28
  settlement and bankruptcy 51
  and wills 25-26
  See also house
property rights:
  and common-law spouses 8-9
  and non-romantic couples 11
property tax deferral programs 106
Provident Life & Accident Insurance 86
provincial law, and family property 42-43

Q

QPP (Quebec Pension Plan) 17
  pension-splitting 45-46
Quebec:
  and common-law unions 9
  financial planners in 119
  and intestacy rules 65
  and joint bank accounts 100
  and living wills 73
  student loans 166

Students Financial Aid 167
tuition fees deduction 171
Quebec Pension Plan *See* QPP

R

real estate 42
ownership in U.S. 107
prices and separation 45
Registered Financial Planner (R.F.P.) 120
relationships, and financial issues 3
religious instruction, of children 8, 9
remarriage *See* marriage and remarriage
Remarriage and Your Money: Once Again for Richer or Poorer (Estess) 52, 56
rental property, tax benefit of 169
replacement cost, insurance 90-91
RESPs (Registered Education Savings Plans) 148-55
how to compare plans 153-55
pooled plans 150
sales tactics for 152
self-directed 153
Revenue Canada 40, 50, 52, 83, 99, 110, 111, 155
reverse mortgages 103-105
Reynolds, Nancy Thalia 132
Rhodes, Ann 108
right of renewal 79
Rodgers, Kelly 121
Rowland, Mary 118
Rowland, Susan 22
RRSP (Registered Retirement Savings Plan):
for common-law partner 11
as emergency funds 62-63
group 20-21
spousal 15-16
students and 171-73
and support payments 40
and tax-free rollovers 43-44

S

safety-deposit boxes, and wills 71
sale leaseback plans 106
same-sex couples 10
and adoption 131-32
and health insurance 18
and pension plans 18
and support rights 37
and wills 27-28
"sandwich" generation 95, 117
Saskatchewan Camping Association 135
Saskatchewan, Student Financial Assistance 167
savings accounts, for children 155-56, 180-83
savings, goals for 179
second marriage *See* marriage and remarriage
"second-generation income" 17
secured credit cards 34
Security Life 104
self-employed:
and benefits 18, 20
disability insurance 83-89
and RRSPs 22
and taxation 128, 129
Seniority: In Search of the Best Nursing Homes and Alternative Care in Canada (West) 109
separation 35-42
and cohabitation agreements 9
and family law 5
protecting yourself after 42-43
and RRSPs 22
what to do before 32-35
See also divorce
separation agreement:
financial aspects 33
and your will 27
shared parenting 47-48

"Sharpen Your Pencil: How Much Life Insurance is Enough" (CLHEA) 75
single parents 46-53
  equivalent-to-spouse exemption 171
single-life insurance 23
small business *See* business
Snyder, Chris 183
sole custody 47
spending, styles of 4
splitting the bills, and money management 4
splitting income *See* income splitting
spousal RRSPs 16-17
spousal support 37
  and cohabitation agreement 9
  and divorce 31-32
  and taxation 37-40
  See also child support
stepparents 52-57
  and adoption 133
Stewart, David 4-5
stockbrokers 120-21
stocks:
  and children 184-86
  dummy portfolios 189
  investing in 157-58
stripped bonds 159
students:
  loans 165-66
  tax returns for 170-71
Substitute Decisions Act (Ontario) 72
summer camp 133-36
support *See* child support; spousal support
Supreme Court of Canada (Thibaudeau vs. Revenue Canada) 37, 39
Surviving Divorce: The Everyday Guide for Canadians (Cochrane) 7
Suzuki, David 2

T

Taking Care of Tomorrow: The Canadian Money Book for Prime Time Women (Matthews and Birch) 32
tax:
  credits and deductions 51-52, 110, 170-71
  deferral programs, for property 106, 169
  and disability insurance 83
  and elderly 110-11
  estate 97
  free income for university 165
  how to minimize 11-18, 99
  and money management 5
  returns for students 170-71
  sheltering 150
  U.S. estate 107-08
"Tax Information for People with Disabilities" (Revenue Canada) 111
taxation:
  and child support 37-40, 49-50
  and legal fees 35
  and spousal RRSPs 16
  of support payments 37-40
teenagers, and new stepsiblings 55
tenant insurance 89-90
"Tenant Insurance, Condominium Insurance and You!" (IBC) 91
term insurance 24, 77-79, 80, 82, 160-61
terminal illness, and your will 27-28
theme parks, for holidays 144-45
Thibaudeau, Suzanne 37, 39
Torkin Manes Cohen & Arbus 42
Toronto Stock Exchange 186
Toys 'R' Us 188
TRAC Insurance Services 80

Trace, Ron 5
travel, with children 139-41
travel insurance, and family holidays 138
Travel With Your Children 144
"trillion-dollar windfall" 116
Trust Companies Association of Canada 64, 67
trust companies, as executors 121-22
trustee:
- acting as 122
- and trust income 164

trusts:
- for children 155
- for education 163-65
- and taxation 100, 165

Truth about Funerals, The (Flynn) 112
tuition fee credit 170-71
Two Homes: A Parent's Guide to Joint Custody in Canada (Coulter) 47

U

universal life insurance 24, 77, 160
- and tax rules 161

Universitas Foundation of Canada 150
University Scholarships of Canada 150
- effective return on 153

unmarried couples:
- and cohabitation agreements 5
- and principal residence 12
- and spousal support 37
- tax advantages and disadvantages 12-13

U.S. Internal Revenue Service 107-08

V

vacations *See* holidays
valuables 192
- and insurance 90
- and your will 99

valuator, of pension plans 45
Vanier Institute of the Family 52, 126
Victorian Order of Nurses 109
visitation rights 49-49
Volpe, Peter 99

W

Wade, P.J. 105
Wall Street Journal 24
Walt Disney Co. 184
West, Michelle 109
whole life insurance 24, 77
wills 64-71, 98-101
- and children 191
- cost of 68-69
- divorce and separation 41-42
- guardians of children 54-55
- and insurance trust 40
- intestacy rules 65-66
- marriage and remarriage 25-26
- and same-sex couples 10
- and unmarried couples 10-11

Winter, Ashton 68
women, and financial decisions 3-5
Working Woman 141

Y

Young Investors Club 186
"Your Pension and Your Spouse" (Martorana and Rowland) 22
"yours, mine and ours family" 54
Youth Plan (Canada Life) 160
Yukon, Advanced Education Branch 168